THE THEOLOGY OF REVELATION OF AVERY DULLES 1980–1994

Symbolic Mediation

ROSS A. SHECTERLE

With a Preface by
Avery Dulles, S.J.

Roman Catholic Studies
Volume 8

The Edwin Mellen Press
Lewiston/Queenston/Lampeter

Library of Congress Cataloging-in-Publication Data

Shecterle, Ross A.
  The theology of revelation of Avery Dulles, 1980-1994 : symbolic mediation / Ross A. Shecterle.
      p.   cm. -- (Roman Catholic studies ; v. 8)
  Includes bibliographical references and index.
  ISBN 0-7734-4248-0 (hb : alk. paper)
  1. Revelation--History of doctrines--20th century.   2. Dulles, Avery Robert, 1918--Contributions to doctrines of revelation.
  I. Title. II. Series
BT126.5.S44   1996
231.7'4'092--dc20   95-50929
                                                              CIP

This is volume 8 in the continuing series
Roman Catholic Studies
Volume 8 ISBN 0-7734-4248-0
RCS Series ISBN 0-88946-240-X

A CIP catalog record for this book is available from the British Library.

The Edwin Mellen Press   The Edwin Mellen Press
Box 450   Box 67
Lewiston, New York   Queenston, Ontario
USA 14092-0450   CANADA L0S 1L0

The Edwin Mellen Press, Ltd.
Lampeter, Dyfed, Wales
UNITED KINGDOM SA48 7DY

Printed in the United States of America

THE THEOLOGY OF REVELATION OF AVERY DULLES 1980–1994

Symbolic Mediation

Dedicated To

THE FACULTY OF
SAINT FRANCIS DE SALES SEMINARY
SAINT FRANCIS, WISCONSIN

HUMAN LIFE IS RADICALLY SYMBOLIC.

GERALD O. COLLINS, S.J.
RETRIEVING FUNDAMENTAL THEOLOGY

ACKNOWLEDGMENTS

This work represents the completion of two years of post-graduate studies in theology at the *Katholieke Universiteit te Leuven*. It becomes a springboard for doctoral studies in pastoral counseling/psychology at Loyola College in Maryland. But these two years here have been about much more than academic theology. These years have been about questioning and discovery, inquiry and revelation, wonder and profound awe in the presence of God. I wish to express my warm gratitude to those people who have inspired me, supported me, and called me, beyond myself, to experience the continued blessings of God's presence in my life:

To my Bishop, the Most Reverend Rembert G. Weakland, O.S.B., who, in the name of the people of the Archdiocese of Milwaukee, has expressed his respect and confidence by calling me to these studies so that I may be actively involved in the formation of the future of the Church. To Rev. Andrew Nelson, Rector, and the Faculty at St. Francis de Sales Seminary, to whom this work is dedicated, for their

i

continued encouragement and support throughout my journey to join them on faculty.

To Professor Dr. Terrence Merrigan, my promoter, for his guidance and assistance with my transition into academic life as well as with this work (especially for his gracious contribution to this text through the writing of the Introduction); his profound love for, and commitment to, the Church has been an inspiration for my own commitment as a priest. To Rev. Dr. Avery Dulles, S.J., for his support and encouragement, for the many hours of dialogue during the beginning stages of this project, for the motivation to publish, as well as his profound contribution to this work through the writing of the Preface. To Rev. Dr. Jacques Haers, S.J., for his encouragement and for planting the seed of insight with his continued plea for "balance" in the theological enterprise. To Dr. Paul Lukacs, PhD., Loyola College in Maryland, to whom I am deeply indebted for his generous editorial assistance and guidance with this work. To Tina Lamberti, M.Ed., for her proofreading assistance with this publication. To the people of Leuven and the country of Belgium, for their hospitality and, who, in their own right, have helped me to broaden the horizons of my world view.

To all my colleagues who have fostered in me a sense of critical insight and a desire for knowledge. I am especially grateful to Rev. Douglas Cook, and Rev. Eugene Sylva for helping me keep balance in my life and for supporting me through the more difficult times.

To my friends, both near and far, who have supported me in word and action, with prayer and guidance. To John and Amy Swiertz, my dearest friends. To Rev. Steve Lampe, Rev. Ken Omernick, and Rev. Michael Witczak. To Sr. Rosemarie Klotz, SSSF. To the Family Lemancik, for their ever present love and profound witness of faith. To Joe and Sandy Zak, for the love and support that was always behind the open door in Sint-Genesius-Rode, Belgium. To the Family Krummenacher (Arch, Switzerland), for their welcome and hospitality during the holidays. To Leo Damge, for his continued support and encouragement.

Most importantly, to my family. To my parents, Donald and Lois Shecterle, for their constant love and support, near and far. To my sister and her husband, Janet and Thomas Clark, and their children, Brian and Scott, for their love and commitment to the faith. To my brother and his wife, Brian and Renee Shecterle, and their daughter, Jessica, for their love and letting me "put my feet up." To my brother and his wife, Mark and April Shecterle, and their daughter, Elizabeth, for their love, for keeping me in my place, and for always reminding me of "down home." And finally, to my deceased grandmother, Marie Shecterle, to whom I will remain ever grateful for her love, her example of faith and her support of my commitment to priesthood.

These people, and so many others, are the "community of faith" through which I experience the symbolic self-communication of God.

Pax vobiscum

Leuven, Belgium
May, 1994

Baltimore, Maryland
Feast of Saint Matthew, 1995

FOREWORD

During the fall term of 1986, I was actively engaged in teaching an introductory religion course to freshmen in high school. Throughout the semester the questions that continually surfaced were, in some sense, all linked to the topic of revelation. "Where is God?" "Does God 'still' reveal himself?" "How do I *know* if God is present?" "Why do we worship as a community?" These questions, and so many others, come rather easily. The answers are more difficult.

A glimpse of an answer came to me later in that same year. I was directing a confirmation retreat at which I had asked some of the "elders" of the community to share their experiences of faith with the students. They were to address the question: "Why are you Catholic?" The stories of faith, and the anecdotes of their personal experiences of the divine, captivated the *confirmandi*. They were so transfixed with interest, their curiosity piqued, that the conversation carried on, well into the night. A couple of weeks later, one of the women, who had shared her "story," died suddenly. The students were deeply grieved and each of them attended her funeral. Afterward, I spent some time with them talking about her death and their experience of her on the retreat. The comments startled me. They spoke of the "power" her words had as she told of her faith and the closeness she felt to God. They remembered her pointing to the strength of her faith as flowing from her activities with the community—from prayer and worship to outreach and service to those "less fortunate." The students said they felt different, "changed," and even more curious to search for the God this woman knew and loved. The experience of these students is a part of the answer. This experience provides some of the impetus for this work.

Revelation is commonly understood to serve three roles within the community—namely, to offer a grounding for the faith of a believer; to guide the community, the Church, in its pilgrim journey and mission on earth; and, to offer a basis for theological thought. Moreover, revelation is located at the center of the dynamic interpersonal relationship between humanity and God. The very essence of the communication of the divine presence elicits a quest for, and a response to, God. Faith, it can be said, is, therefore, the response to the self-disclosure of God. Hence, theology, is a systematic reflection upon that faith and that revelation. These suppositions are, most certainly, true for the theologian, Avery Dulles, who has set out to offer new direction and insight into this most important dimension of reality.

This work, therefore, will attempt to offer an exploration on the symbolic structure and mediation of revelation as understood by Dulles: his new direction and insight. It will look at his presuppositions about the nature of human knowing and how this radically affects his development of a theology of revelation. It will address both the social and the symbolic dimensions of revelation, most specifically, in the area of the unique relationship that the self-disclosure of the divine demands. The first chapter deals with Dulles' belief that revelation is foundational for the theological enterprise. It looks at Dulles' presuppositions regarding the significance of revelation for the varying dimensions, and facets, of theology—specifically, the notion of communication and revelation as such. It also offers a survey both of George Lindbeck's categorization of approaches to doctrine and Dulles' "models" of revelation.

The second chapter deals with a critical link perceived between anthropology and theology. Through an appropriation of the work of Karl Rahner, namely Rahner's anthropology and his ontology of symbol, Dulles begins to draw connections between the symbolic nature of the human being and the symbolic mediation of the self-communication of God. We will explore the definition of symbol, set forth by Dulles, along with its constitutive elements. A clear understanding of the symbol will offer Dulles the opportunity to draw some connections between symbolic knowledge and revelation. Here, the influence of Michael Polanyi on Dulles, namely, his notion of "indwelling" and participatory knowledge, will be surfaced.

The third chapter is an in-depth exploration of symbol and revelation. Dulles will draw a parallel between the nature of symbol and the symbolic character of revelation. The notions of Polanyi find strong grounding here. Polanyi's notion of "indwelling," blended with John Henry Newman's notion of the *sensus fidelium*, and situated in a profound Dullesian interest in the notion of "discovery," will constitute a critical framework for Dulles' enterprise. The dynamics of the interaction of these notions become significant as Dulles attempts to formulate a fresh approach to revelation.

The final chapter takes a look at Dulles' approach to revelation, the "ecclesial-transformative" approach. Dulles re-defines George Lindbeck's own theory of doctrine, namely, the "cultural-linguistic" theory. His aim is to offer an approach to revelation, and theology as a whole, that will address his belief that, the system of theology espoused by the neo-scholastics, does not sufficiently address, or, for that matter, acknowledge, the "personalist, symbolic, and mystical dimensions of faith." This approach, in turn, opens up the possibility for new life and conversion, transformation, as it were, of the church and its members. This is Dulles' goal. Finally, this chapter offers some concluding evaluative comments, as well as critique, of Dulles' thought and this symbolic theological enterprise.

Dulles' work on the symbolic mediation of the self-communication of God invites the members of the community of faith to appreciate the active, dynamic, and creative presence of God in their midst. It calls the faithful, in turn, to re-evaluate their unique role in the on-going, re-expression, of their experiences of God. Dulles' considerations, if they are engendered in the life of faith of the community, can, as he suspects, truly be transformative—for the individual, the community and the world. The aim of this project is to identify the substantial contribution of Dulles' symbolic notion of revelation to theology.

CONTENTS

ACKNOWLEDGMENTS...i
FOREWORD...v
CONTENTS xi
ABBREVIATIONS xv
PREFACE...xvii
INTRODUCTION by Terrence Merrigan xix

CHAPTER ONE The Relevance of the Topic of Revelation
  Revelation as Foundational for the Whole of Theology...........1
    A Brief History of the Idea of Revelation............................1
    Revelation as Fundamental for all Theology........................6
    Revelation and George Lindbeck's Categorization of
          Theories of Doctrine 19
      An Analysis of the Traditional Approaches to Doctrine 20
      The Cultural-Linguistic Theory of Doctrine....................23
    An Overview of Dulles and His Models of Revelation 30
      The Propositional or Doctrinal Model of Revelation 31
      The Historical Model of Revelation................................32
      The Mystical or Inner Experience Model of Revelation..33
      The Dialectical Model of Revelation...............................35
      The New Awareness Model of Revelation.......................37
    Some Concluding Remarks..39

CHAPTER TWO Anthropological Considerations and the
          Significance of Symbol
  Anthropology and Symbol..41
    Critical Elements of Anthropology.....................................41
    A Definition of the Human Being 46
    The Significance of Symbol and Symbolism 50

The Nature of Symbol...56
  Participatory Knowledge...................................57
  Transformative Effects......................................59
  Influence on Commitments and Behaviors..................60
  New Realms of Awareness.................................61
The Symbolic Structure of Reality within the Context
  of Anthropology..65
Communication and Language as Integral to the
  Human Being 68
Communication and the Transmission of Symbol...........71
  Language as Socially, Culturally, and
    Historically Conditioned 76
  Language, Word and Gesture, as Symbol 76
  Revelation and Language..................................78
Communication as Inherent to a Methodological Approach
  to Revelation..81

CHAPTER THREE Revelation and Symbol
Symbolic Communication and the Divine 85
The Symbolic Character of Revelation.......................85
  An Understanding of Symbolic Language and
    Revelation...87
    Participatory Awareness.................................88
    Transformative Effects....................................90
    Impact on Commitments and Conduct...................91
    Insight into Mysteries....................................93
God's Self–Disclosure and Symbolic Realism...............97
  Symbolic Realism—Faith as an Openness to Symbol ...101
  Social and Symbolic Dimensions of the Divine
    Self-Communication 112
    The Social Dimensions of Revelation...................115
    The Symbolic Dimensions of Revelation 117

Conversion as the Transformative Element of
  Revelation..118
Knowledge and Understanding Realized........................121
Reception and Knowledge of Revelation 128
  Indwelling..129
  Sensus Fidelium..136
Christ as the Symbolic Whole of God's Self-Disclosure..144

CHAPTER FOUR Dulles and an Ecclesial-Transformative
  Approach to Revelation
An Ecclesial-Transformative Doctrine of Revelation...........155
A Redefinition of Lindbeck's "Cultural-Linguistic"
  Category...155
  A Process of "Socialization" - The Individual 159
  "Traditioning" and the *Ecclesia* - The Community 166
Scripture, Tradition, Magisterium 173
  The Sacred Scriptures...175
  Tradition, tradition and traditions.................................180
  The Teaching Authority of the Church..........................187
Ten Theses Paradigmatic of the
  Ecclesial-Transformative Approach..............................191
Evaluation and Critique of Dulles' Thought 194
  Some Concerns..194
  Some Benefits..203
Postscript..205

SELECTED BIBLIOGRAPHY 209
INDEX...221

ABBREVIATIONS

DF   *Dei Filius* (Vatican I's Constitution on the Catholic Faith)

DS   *Enchiridion Symbolorum, Definitionum et Declarationum de Rebus Fidei et Morum*

DV   *Dei Verbum* (Vatican II's Constitution on Divine Revelation)

GS   *Gaudium et Spes* (Vatican II's Pastoral Constitiution on the Church in the Modern World)

LG   *Lumen Gentium* (Vatican II's Constitution on the Church)

PL   *Patrologia Latina*

SC   *Sacrosanctum Concilium* (Vatican II's Constitution on the Sacred Liturgy)

PREFACE

In these pages Ross Shecterle gives a lucid and accurate presentation of my essential thinking on revelation and symbolic communication. In so doing he takes up one of the central themes of my work since I began to teach theology in 1960. He concentrates quite properly on my work since 1980, which is surely the best place for the reader or student to begin. I believe that in these more recent writings I have incorporated the key insights expressed in my earlier writings.

A particular value in this study is the author's ability to go right to the heart of the matter without getting lost in details or distracted by side issues. Father Shecterle rightly emphasizes the "ecclesial transformative" approach to revelation as being central to my thought. Without neglecting my other writings, he integrates themes taken from two of my recent books, *Models of Revelation* and *The Craft of Theology*. For those who would profit from a descriptive and critical introduction to these works, this study may be confidently recommended.

I am highly flattered to be the subject of this penetrating study. Because Father Shecterle is so generous in his evaluation, I feel that no response on my part is needed. His few criticisms, set forth with great moderation in his final chapter, raise questions which could not be adequately handled in a brief preface of this kind. I hope to be able to profit from Shecterle's criticisms in any future work I may do on the subject.

Although the book deals with my work, it has broader significance and is a substantive contribution to the theology of revelation. It should be of interest to many who are looking for light on the nature and mediation of revelation— themes surely central to Christian faith and existence. In some respects Ross Shecterle's presentation of these themes is more compact and trenchant than my own, since he is able to bring together in brief compass the best fruits of my own laborious and heavily footnoted investigations. He and his mentors at the *Katholieke Universiteit Leuven* are to be congratulated on this attractive piece of work. I am pleased that The Edwin Mellen Press is including this book in its Roman Catholic Studies Series on contemporary theology.

Avery Dulles, S.J.

INTRODUCTION

REVELATION AND ITS MEDIATION
THE CONTRIBUTION OF AVERY DULLES

The Problem with Revelation

In George Bernard Shaw's celebrated play, *Saint Joan*, one of Joan's interrogators chides her that the voices she claims to hear directing her, and which she regards as divine, come from her "imagination." Unabashed, Joan replies, "Of course. That is how the messages of God come to us."[1] In answering in this fashion, Shaw's Joan displays genuine theological insight. There can be no divine revelation without some form of human mediation. To inquire into the character of revelation is to inquire into the fashion in which we come to know it. The category of mediation is essential to the discussion of revelation.

In a recent study, the British theologian, Colin Gunton, observes that, since the time of Hegel, theology has sought to account for the contents of so-called 'revealed' religion by the appeal to "different forms of immediacy." As cases in point,

---

[1] Bernard Shaw, *Saint Joan: A Chronicle Play in Six Scenes and an Epilogue*, Penguin Books (Harmondsworth, England: Penguin Books, 1979), 59.

Gunton refers to Hegel's view that "revelation is the function of an immediate relation of God to the mind," and Schleiermacher's claim that "religion is a form of immediacy to experience." Gunton observes that even there where the traditional notion of a distinctive historical revelation is retained such as, for example, in fundamentalist theology, but also in "the recent fashion for narrative or intratextuality," there is often "a seeking of what can only be called a revelatory immediacy, a direct apprehension of the content of the faith that will in some way or other serve to identify it beyond question."[2]

The bitter confessional history of Christianity does not encourage the view that the content of faith can ever be the object of direct apprehension. The "messages of God" are neither immediately discernible nor easily decipherable. Shaw's Joan is told by the Inquisitor that her "revelations and visions are sent by the devil," a view which she herself briefly endorses before returning to her conviction that they are divinely inspired. The latter interpretation came to be the view of the Church. More than five hundred years after she had first heard her "voices," St. Joan of Arc was canonized in 1920.[3]

---

[2] Colin Gunton, *A Brief Theology of Revelation* (Edinburgh: T & T Clark, 1995), 3-5.

[3] Shaw, *Saint Joan*, 129, 134, 155.

Revelation in Contemporary Pluralist Theology

In our time, the theme of "revelatory immediacy" is, if anything, even more alive than in Hegel's day. The pluralist theology of religions, with its proposition of the essential parity of the world's great "post-axial" religious traditions,[4] is clearly an extension of the Enlightenment quest to ground all religion on the secure foundation of universal reason.

Pluralist theology, so to speak, extends the revelatory franchise to all the great post-axial traditions. From the pluralist perspective, the world's religious traditions represent the culturally-conditioned expressions of a universally accessible religious experience.[5] That experience is, of course, always shaped by the cultural and religious context within which it finds place. In this sense, there is no such thing as "pure" religious experience, and pluralists rightly reject the charge that they regard particular religious traditions as, so to speak, "accessories after the religious fact." The concrete religious traditions provide the forum within which religious experience becomes possible, and the categories which allow believers both to express that

---

[4] John Hick borrows this term from the work of Karl Jaspers, who spoke of the "*Achsenzeit*", to describe the period between 800 and 200 B.C., when an evolution found place "from archaic religion to the religions of salvation or liberation." See John Hick, *An Interpretation of Religion: Human Responses to the Transcendent* (London: Macmillan, 1989), 29-33.

[5] See, for example, John Hick, *An Interpretation of Religion*, 14; *The Metaphor of God Incarnate* (London: SCM, 1993), 38-39.

experience and, most importantly, to identify its source or its ground.

Christianity, like every particular religious tradition, provides us with a qualified "knowledge" of the religious object. It is in the interest of every tradition that its qualified "knowledge" be supplemented, if not corrected, by the insights of other traditions. Once the partial character of all truth-claims has been established, the problem of rival truth-claims can be readily addressed. As far as the religious object itself is concerned, such claims are best regarded as complementary. (This issues in a view of religious truth as polar).[6] As far as the reciprocal relations among the world's religious traditions are concerned, dialogue presents itself as the only rationally and religiously defensible option. (This issues in an appeal to believers in all traditions to engage in the practice of "crossing-over" from one tradition to another).[7] As far as the reconciliation

---

[6] Regarding the polar character of religious truth, see, for example, Raimundo Panikkar, "The Jordan, the Tiber and the Ganges: Three Kairological Moments of Christic Self-Consciousness," in *The Myth of Christian Uniqueness*, eds. J. Hick and P. Knitter (Maryknoll, NY: Orbis, 1988), 102, 103, 110; Paul Knitter, *No Other Name? A Critical Attitude Survey of Christian Attitudes Toward the World Religions* (Maryknoll, NY: 1985), 220. In an article which appeared in 1990, "Interreligious Dialogue: What? Why? How?," in *Death or Dialogue? From the Age of Monologue to the Age of Dialogue* (London: SCM, 1990), 20-21, Knitter acknowledges that the differences among the world's religions are greater than he had previously suggested. In this context, one must take the existing situation of plurality as the point of departure "before we can ever contemplate, much less realize, their possible unity or oneness."

[7] Regarding the theme of "crossing-over," see Knitter, *No Other Name?*, 53, 209, 210, 212, 213.

of rival doctrinal traditions is concerned, believers are invited to tolerate differences, to acknowledge the ultimately mysterious character of the religious object, and to recognize that all religions are already united in sharing a common soteriological concern, namely, "the realization of a limitlessly better possibility" of human existence through the promotion of "the transformation of human existence from self-centredness to Reality-centredness."[8] (This issues in the so-called soteriocentric approach to interreligious dialogue, that is to say, the determination to focus not on doctrinal differences but on the concrete project of human liberation).[9]

Pluralist theology is united in its insistence that the object of humanity's religious project — variously identified as God, the Absolute, or the Real, etc., — is susceptible of apprehension in and through a variety of religious and cultural media, which are themselves subject to the permutations of history. In other words, pluralist theology regards God or the Absolute primarily as the always elusive object of human religious experience and humanity's historical religious quest. It

---

[8] Hick, *An Interpretation of Religion*, 12, 14. See also John Hick, "Interpretation and Reinterpretation in Religion," in *The Making and Remaking of Christian Doctrine: Essays in Honour of Maurice Wiles*, eds. S. Coakley and D. A. Pailin (Oxford: Clarendon, 1993), 69.

[9] Paul Knitter's recent theology has tended to concentrate on the soteriocentric approach to interreligious dialogue. See his "Toward a Liberation Theology of Religions," in *The Myth of Christian Uniqueness*, 178-200; "A Liberation-Centered Theology of Religions," *The Drew Gateway* 58 (1988), 22-29.

regards the Christian tradition of faith as a human construct, a cultural artifact born out of profound human experiences and expressive of a (more or less) timeless wisdom which can serve us in our ongoing quest for meaning. This same theology holds that it is the task of the church to share this wisdom with humankind, as humanity attempts to come to terms with a new social and religious order. The wisdom of the past is to be assessed in the light of its relevance to the present, a present which is increasingly characterized by a far-reaching pluralism. Within the framework of pluralist theology, the prevailing social and intellectual context acquires unprecedented *theological* significance.[10] Traditional doctrine is to be reevaluated in the light of contemporary cultural shifts.

The Mediation of Historical Revelation: The Teaching of Vatican II

The question of how revelation finds place, and the problem of its relationship to the context within which it finds expression are central to the contemporary theology of revelation. Pluralist theology's response to both these issues is clear. Revelation is to be conceived in terms of experiential

---

[10] The authors who contributed to *The Myth of Christian Uniqueness* were invited "to formulate their views on why they felt the contemporary context was pressing Christians toward a new pluralist approach toward other religions." See p. ix.

immediacy, and the contemporary context is to be accorded a determinant role in defining its content.

This represents a radical departure from the traditional Catholic understanding of revelation, which locates the heart of the revelatory event in the contingent history of Jesus of Nazareth, and insists on the necessary mediatory role of the apostolically constituted Church and its authoritative tradition of faith. Especially since Vatican II, the Catholic theology of revelation has sought to elaborate both these themes in a fashion which does justice to the modern sensibility to human experience and the modern awareness of the historically conditioned character of all human discourse.

In the *Dogmatic Constitution on Divine Revelation, Dei Verbum*, "the first conciliar document on God's self-revelation . . . in the history of Christianity,"[11] the Fathers of the Second Vatican Council attempted to "set forth authentic teaching on God's revelation and how it is communicated" (*Dei Verbum*, no. 1). The Constitution clearly conceives of that revelation primarily in christological terms. Indeed, *Dei Verbum* has been described as "thoroughly christocentric, since it recognizes the climax of revelation and its signs in the death and resurrection of God's incarnate Son — with their outcome in the sending of Christ's Holy Spirit through whom the revelation given once and

---

[11] Gerald O'Collins, *Retrieving Fundamental Theology: The Three Styles of Contemporary Theology* (New York: Paulist, 1993), 57.

for all remains a present reality."[12] This christocentric focus is reflected in the fact that, whereas Vatican I had spoken of revelation in terms of the divine "mysteries" (in the plural), *Dei Verbum* employs only the singular and refers to either "the mystery" or "the mystery of Christ" (a genitive of identification or definition, meaning the mystery that is Christ).[13]

From the outset, *Dei Verbum* equates God's revelatory activity with His salvific activity. In the words of Gerald O'Collins, "the plan or 'economy of revelation' is synonymous with the 'history of salvation.'" *Dei Verbum* continually moves between the language of salvation and revelation. These are "two inseparable, if distinguishable, realities," the "two inseparable dimensions of God's self-communication."[14]

The idea of revelation as the divine "self-communication" represents a significant development in official teaching. This is not to suggest that it was entirely unprepared. The First Vatican Council (1870), which was characterized by a cognitivist approach to divine revelation, had nevertheless insisted that it had pleased God to "reveal *Himself* and the eternal decrees of

---

[12] O'Collins, *Retrieving Fundamental Theology*, 48. O'Collins (p. 56) notes that *Dei Verbum* "illustrates a Latin tendency to subordinate the work of the Spirit to that of the Son." "If the Second Vatican Council had met in the 1990s," he comments, "the Holy Spirit would have bulked larger in *Dei Verbum*."

[13] O'Collins, *Retrieving Fundamental Theology*, 26, 51, 73.

[14] O'Collins, *Retrieving Fundamental Theology*, 54, 73. See *Dei Verbum*, nos. 2, 3, 4, 6, 7, 14-15, 17, 21.

His will" (*Dei Filius*, ch. 2). *Dei Verbum*, no. 6 cited these words of *Dei Filius*, but replaced the word "reveal" by two other words, namely "manifest and communicate" ("*manifestare ac communicare*"). The final text of *Dei Verbum* 6 now reads as follows: "By divine revelation God has chosen to manifest and communicate both Himself and the eternal decrees of His will for the salvation of humankind." O'Collins makes much of the introduction of the word "communication" into *Dei Verbum*. In his view, this usage marked the entry of "the language of the divine 'communication' and eventually God's 'self-communication'" into "official Catholic teaching." "The peculiar value of the term," O'Collins writes, "comes from the way it can hold together God's self-*revelation* and self-*giving* through saving grace. God's communication is not merely cognitive but constitutes a *real* self-communication of God which not only makes salvation known but actually brings it in person."[15] *In Dei Verbum* and elsewhere, the Council makes it clear that God's self-revelation ("*sese revelans*") culminates in the history of Jesus Christ. *Gaudium et Spes*, no. 58 speaks, in this regard, of God "showing Himself fully in the incarnate Son."[16]

It is no exaggeration to say that the conciliar documents in general and *Dei Verbum* in particular appear to support the view that christology is the key to the doctrine of revelation.

---

[15] O'Collins, *Retrieving Fundamental Theology*, 53.

[16] See *Dei Verbum*, nos. 4, 14-15, 17; *Lumen Gentium*, no. 5; *Gaudium et Spes*, no. 58; *Ad Gentes*, no. 3 n. 2.

Nevertheless, the *Dogmatic Constitution on Divine Revelation*, despite its title, offers us little in the way of a theology of revelation. Despite its promise to "set forth authentic teaching on God's revelation and how it is communicated" (no. 1), it devotes only the first of its six chapters to "revelation itself" and then turns its entire attention to the question of the transmission of revelation.

However, what at first sight appears to be a reason for dismay, is, on closer inspection, an enlightening and, above all, a promising development. *Dei Verbum* and the other conciliar documents, in directing their attention especially to the way in which revelation is transmitted, have, in fact, told us much about its character and its content. By clarifying the way in which the central Christian mystery, the person and work of Christ, is communicated, they have illuminated its particular content. To put it another way, the Council's approach to revelation makes it clear that, *in the case of Christian revelation, the medium (of transmission) is very much the message.*

In a most daring passage, the *Dogmatic Constitution on the Church, Lumen Gentium*, portrays the Church's role in the world by means of an "analogy" (*analogiam*) with the Incarnation: "For just as the assumed nature serves the divine Word as a living instrument of salvation inseparably joined with him, in a similar way the social structure of the church serves the Spirit of Christ . . ." (no. 8). It is the task of the visible Church community to "reveal Christ" (*Ad Gentes*, no. 8), to serve as "a living instrument of salvation" (*vivum organum salutis*). As we have seen, according to the Council's teaching, these two concerns, i.e., revelation and salvation, are indivisible. They are the two inseparable dimensions of God's self-communication.

It is the fusion of both these dimensions which accounts for the dynamic notion of tradition developed by the Council, and according to which tradition is no longer a static quantity of revealed truths but the "Verbum Dei traditum" (no. 10), that is to say, the dynamic process of witnessing to Christ (no. 9). As far as this witness is concerned, *Dei Verbum* is most suggestive when it asserts that "the church, in its *teaching, life and worship*, perpetuates and hands on to every generation all that it is and all that it believes" (no. 8). It is not difficult, on the basis of this text, to describe Christian tradition (and revelation) as encompassing teaching (knowledge/cognition), praxis (action/discipleship) and worship (prayer/spirituality).[17]

Dei Verbum itself, by focussing on Scripture and the apostolic office (nos. 7-10, 12, 21-26), tends to highlight the cognitive dimension of tradition and, to a lesser extent, its link with the Church's life of worship. The other conciliar documents develop and go beyond *Dei Verbum's* teaching.

It is especially in its treatment of the revelatory value of Christian witness, as an element of tradition, that the Council opens up new vistas for the theology of revelation, and provides

---

[17] I am indebted to O'Collins for this insight. See his *Retrieving Fundamental Theology*, 9-13; 154 nn. 5,6; 165 n. 7.

us with an opening to address the themes of experience and our age. In our age (and, indeed, in every age), this witness is rendered more effectively in life and worship, than in teaching.

The conciliar documents provide a number of interesting reflections on the church's role as mediator of revelation, as mediator of Christ. The *Constitution on the Sacred Liturgy* insists that Christ is "present through his power in the sacraments," especially the Eucharist, as well as in his word, and in the church's prayer (nos. 7, 33). On other occasions, the church's missionary and pastoral activity are said to manifest Christ.[18] Indeed, *Ad Gentes* declares that "missionary activity is nothing other and nothing less than the manifestation or epiphany of God's plan and its fulfillment in the world and in its history; in this history, by means of missions, God clearly accomplishes the history of salvation" (no. 9). Elsewhere, the office of bishops is described as one of "witness" to the revealed truth (*Lumen Gentium*, no. 25).

In *Ad Gentes*, we read that Christians are called "by the example of their lives and the witness of the word" to "manifest" (*manifestare*) Christ (no. 11). *Lumen Gentium* declares that "God makes vividly manifest to humanity his presence and his face" in "the lives of those who, while sharing our humanity, are nevertheless more perfectly transformed into the image of Christ

---

[18] See *Lumen Gentium*, nos. 15, 48; *Ad Gentes*, nos. 8, 9, 11, 12; *Gaudium et Spes*, nos. 10, 11, 41, 45.

(see 2 Cor 3:18)" (no. 50).[19] Picking up on a theme contained in a number of conciliar texts, *Gaudium et Spes* describes the church as the "universal sacrament of salvation" which, through the "good" it contributes to the human family, "shows forth and at the same time brings into effect the mystery of God's love for humanity" (no. 45). The Council clearly identifies "love" as the heart of the Christian revelation, and just as clearly enjoins the practice of love on Christians in imitation of Christ. For the Council, the practice of love is not merely a response to revealed truth, but the realization of that truth in history, in "the world of today." At this point, the radically historical and hence alarmingly vulnerable character of Christian revelation becomes apparent. *Where Christian witness is not forthcoming, God ceases to speak.*

Revelation and its Mediation in the Theology of Avery Dulles

Among those Catholic theologians who have sought to develop the fundamental insights of Vatican II on revelation and its transmission, Avery Dulles occupies a special place. It is difficult to find another theologian who has so consistently and so comprehensively situated revelation where it belongs, namely, in the heart of the believing community which revelation calls into being and which exists to bear witness to that revelation.

---

[19] This text is used with reference to the saints, but clearly need not be restricted only to those whose virtue has been officially acknowledged.

Dulles shares the christological focus developed by the Council. His Christ, however, is only accessible via the mediation of the living community of faith which both treasures his memory and experiences him as its present Lord. As he observes in one of his essays, "God's revelation, if it is to come home to human beings as embodied spirits, must come to expression through tangible, social, and historically transmitted symbols."[20] Primary among these symbols is, of course, Christ himself, the "unsurpassable symbol," who continues to "make himself present through word and sacrament" which are "constitutive of the Church."[21] For Dulles, revelation is symbolic mediation and symbolic mediation is the *raison d'être* of the Church. The Church lives *from* symbols and lives *to* symbolize, that is to say, it is founded on Christ and exists to "extend in space and time the physical body of the Lord. It is not a mere pointer to the absent Christ, but the symbolic manifestation of the present Christ."[22]

Throughout his writings, Dulles insists that knowledge of revelation is only possible through participation in the faith tradition of the believing community. In stressing this theme,

---

[20] Avery Dulles, "Theology and Symbolic Communication," in *The Craft of Theology: From Symbol to System*, revised edition (New York: Crossroad, 1995), 22.

[21] Dulles, *The Craft of Theology*, 27, 33.

[22] Avery Dulles, "Faith and Revelation," in *Systematic Theology: Roman Catholic Perspectives*, 2 vols., eds. Francis Schüssler Fiorenza and John P. Galvin (Minneapolis: Fortress, 1991), 1:117.

Dulles is reiterating the "classical" principle of the *sensus fidelium*, that is to say, the view that immersion in the revelatory tradition enables the believer to acquire "a kind of connaturality or connoisseurship that enables one to judge what is or is not consonant with revelation." Dulles acknowledges that his approach to theology "gives new vitality to classical theological loci such as the 'sense of the faithful.'" He repeatedly alludes to the work of Michael Polanyi and John Henry Newman[23] to develop his view that "the contents of faith are known not by merely detached observation but by indwelling or participation." Theology, too, as a "methodical effort to articulate the truth implied in Christian faith, the faith of the Church, . . . cannot be pursued by the techniques of mathematics or syllogistic logic, but . . . depends on a kind of connoisseurship derived from personal appropriation of the living faith of the Church."[24]

Dulles insists that while Christians might disagree as far as their "concepts" of revelation are concerned, they nevertheless share a common "fund of tacit knowledge," an implicit communal perception, as it were, of the "reality" of revelation which the concepts seek to clarify.[25] He describes this shared perception as

---

[23] I have discussed Dulles' appeal to Polanyi and Newman in "Models in the Theology of Avery Dulles: A Critical Analysis," *Bijdragen* 54 (1993), 141-161.

[24] Dulles, "Toward a Post-Critical Theology," in *The Craft of Theology*, 9, 8.

[25] Avery Dulles, *Models of Revelation* (Maryknoll: Orbis, 1992), 116-117.

a "certain prethematic awareness," a "personal contact" which is "given to all in faith." Elsewhere he speaks of the "vital indwelling" of the believer in the "reality of revelation" and of a "real existential" or "lived" relationship between the believer and the subject of revelation.[26] The tacit or "implicit" knowledge generated by this "indwelling" or "lived relationship" enables the one enjoying it to assess the adequacy of particular theories of revelation.[27] The believer, to use Polanyi's words, "knows more than he or she can tell."[28]

Dulles affirms that "the fruits of the process [of God's self-revelation], 'objectively' contained in Scripture and tradition, are transmitted to believers by education in the church, the living community of faith." "By participation in the community of faith the individual believer can have reliable access to the revelatory meaning of the signs and symbols through which God's self-disclosure has taken place and through which God's salvific designs have been made known."[29] Recalling

---

[26] Dulles, *Models of Revelation*, 128, 127, 144.

[27] Dulles, *Models of Revelation*, viii, 127: "A theory of revelation is sound and acceptable to the extent that it measures up to, and illuminates, the reality of revelation."

[28] Michael Polanyi, *Personal Knowledge* (New York: Harper & Row, Harper Torchbook, 1962), x. See Dulles, *Models of Revelation*, viii: "All Christian believers, it could be said, tacitly know what revelation is simply by virtue of adherence to a revealed religion. But they do not yet have a formulated concept or theory of revelation."

[29] Dulles, "Faith and Revelation," 1:94, 98.

Vatican II's teaching that revelation comes to expression in all dimensions of the church's life, her witness and worship no less than her teaching, Dulles observes that "authentic tradition is to be found not only in formal statements but also in 'the practice and life of the believing and praying Church.'"[30]

This sensitivity to the whole life and practice of the Church is characteristic of Dulles and marks him out as one of the most important representatives of the theology of Vatican II. However, even this description does not do him justice. In an article written in 1991, David Tracy insisted that "the category 'mediation' is central to the Catholic understanding of all reality."[31] Seen in the light of this claim, Dulles' theology of symbolic mediation stands as one of the most comprehensive Catholic theologies on the contemporary scene. It is the great merit of Father Ross Shecterle that he has made this theology even more accessible to all who are concerned with the ongoing witness to Christ.

Terrence Merrigan
Katholieke Universiteit
Leuven Belgium

---

[30] Dulles, "Faith and Revelation," 1:121. See also Dulles' "Tradition as a Theological Source," in *The Craft of Theology*, 103.

[31] David Tracy, "Approaching the Christian Understanding of God," in *Systematic Theology*, 1:134, 136, and n. 10.

CHAPTER ONE
THE RELEVANCE OF THE TOPIC OF REVELATION

Revelation as Foundational for the Whole of Theology

A Brief History of the Idea of Revelation

Since the beginning of human history every civilization has investigated ultimate questions regarding the foundation of reality and the meaning of humanity's place in that reality. These investigations often have taken the form of questions about deity. Specialists and non-specialists have engaged, and continue to engage, in an attempt to open up the world of the transcendent order and then to locate the strands of some relationship that might connect that order with the empirical order of daily human life.

The great Western religions—Judaism, Christianity, and Islam—are based on the

conviction that the existence of the world and the
final meaning and value of all that it contains
ultimately depend on a personal God who, while
distinct from the world and everything in it, is
absolute in terms of reality, goodness, and power.
These religions profess to derive their
fundamental vision not from mere human
speculation, which would be tentative and
uncertain, but from God's own testimony—that
is to say, from a historically given divine
revelation.[1]

Within the Christian tradition, this "historically given divine
revelation" is characterized as a permanently valid revelation that
was given to humanity by God. Its content concerns God and
God's relationship to the world and its creatures. As revelation,

---

[1]Avery Dulles, *Models of Revelation* (New York:
Doubleday, 1983; new edition, Maryknoll: Orbis, 1992), 3. [All
references to *Models of Revelation* will be to the 1992 edition. This
edition's new preface is the only significant difference from the
1983 edition.].

"If there are two ultimate questions in human life—who, or
what is God? and who, or what, are we?—revelation may be seen as
God's answer to both of them. [And], unlike other answers to more
limited questions, this one does not put and end to the
questioning—though it reorients it, giving it both a new direction
and the assurance of finding its goal." See Justin J. Kelly, "Knowing
by Heart: The Symbolic Structure of Revelation and Faith," in
Faithful Witness: Foundations of Theology for Today's Church, ed.
Leo J. O'Donovan and T. Howland Sanks (New York: Crossroad,
1989), 83.

it has been documented throughout the biblical era through the lives of Moses and the prophets, and it attains its fullest expression in Jesus Christ. "The Christian church down through the centuries has been committed to this revelation and has sought to propagate it, defend it, and explain its implications."[2]

Although the Christian church has been "committed" to the idea of God's revelation being ultimately grounded in Jesus Christ and God's relationship to humanity through Jesus, revelation *per se* did not always hold a position of prominence in the theological enterprise of the church. Only sometime near the end of the nineteenth century did the Christian churches become "equipped with a systematically complete doctrine of revelation as a deposit of truth built up in biblical times and reliably transmitted through the Bible and Church teachings."[3] Prior to this period, revelation in and of itself was basically "taken for granted" and presupposed in the life of the church. It was only through a need to respond to a developing heresy or articulate and justify a particular confessional stance that the idea of revelation was even addressed. Today, near the close of the twentieth century, the idea of revelation as a "permanently valid body of truths" communicated to humanity by God within the historical, biblical era is still generally accepted within the

---

[2]Dulles, *Models of Revelation,* 3.
[3]Dulles, *Models of Revelation,* 4.

Christian tradition. It remains, however, a focal point of debate and question.[4]

Some of the present difficulties that surround the idea of God's revelation include questions about the *content* of

---

[4]For an exploration of the contemporary difficulties and questions surrounding the idea of revelation, see Avery Dulles, *Models of Revelation*, 6-8. Dulles notes, however, that his presentation of these difficulties (he lists eight) is by no means exhaustive.

Dulles identifies the following difficulties: philosophical agnosticism (Can human reason go beyond the phenomenon of worldly experience?); linguistic analysis (This area addresses the paradoxical/symbolic character of God-talk and raises a question concerning language about the divine asking if it possesses any definitive cognitive content.); modern epistemology (Dulles believes that this subverts the distinction between revealed and acquired knowledge. It holds that all human knowledge *must* be acquired by the individual and be subject to the limitations of the human subject.); empirical psychology (This discipline, Dulles contends, eliminates all possibility for "visions and auditions" received within a prophetic framework by discrediting them with suggestions of "drug" usage and the frailty of the human psyche.); biblical criticism (The question biblical criticism raises bespeaks the difficulty: Is it possible to attribute "revealed" information to a divine agency?); the history of Christian doctrine (What has been understood as "revealed" truth has been "reclassified"—for example, the Copernican theories of planetary rotation and, more recently, the "papal pardon" of Galileo in October, 1992.); studies in comparative religion (Inherent and explicit claims of contrary revelation or an articulation of the non-existence of revelation present problems that need to be addressed.); and critical sociology (This discipline addresses the ideological component of any belief system.).

revelation and its *mediation*, along with questions concerning the *re-transmission* of revelation within the faith tradition of a community of believers. Two points need to be stated. First, what gave rise to the current debate is, essentially, a stalemate. There are those who believe that "nothing else" need be said. Revelation has been, and is, "permanently valid." Clearly, however, this is an inadequate view of the matter. The revelation that was "given once, for all" has been the subject of continued discussion and debate throughout the centuries and such discussion goes on. But this raises the second point. Those who enter the discussion, those who are willing to grapple with the difficult questions in search of a deeper, more refined and inherently meaningful understanding of God's revelatory discourse with humanity, inevitably enter the dialogue from a particular tradition.

> The Jewish-Christian view of God, the world, and human life is inseparably intertwined with the conviction that God is free and personal, that he acts on behalf of those whom he loves, and that his action includes, already within history, a partial disclosure of his nature, attributes, attitudes, and intentions.[5]

---

[5]Dulles, *Models of Revelation,* 13.

Within the Roman Catholic context, this particular tradition provides the framework for Dulles' view of revelation as foundational for the whole theological enterprise.

This is the context within which the thought of Avery Dulles operates. He contends that "once the approach to revelation has been clarified in fundamental theology, there remains the task of studying revelation in the context of a total theological system."[6] He argues that revelation is central to all of theology. Moreover, he argues that revelation is inherently symbolic—a kind of symbolic communication. The result is an "ecclesial-transformative" approach to revelation and theology. The following discussion is dedicated to the consideration of such a system.

Revelation as Fundamental for all Theology

One of Dulles' more recent works, *The Craft of Theology*, addresses the relationship between communication and theology.[7] Dulles points out that, historically, the enterprise of

---

[6]Dulles, *Models of Revelation,* xx, ix: Dulles believes that "theology cannot maintain its identity and vigor if it overlooks this foundational category." He argues for a restoration of revelation as a primary theological category.

[7]Avery Dulles, *The Craft of Theology: From Symbol to System* (New York: Crossroad, 1992; Expanded Edition, 1995), 21 [All references to *The Craft of Theology* will be to the 1992 edition unless specifically noted. The expanded edition involves two
Continued on next page

theology has been focused mainly on its "formal object," which he defines as "who" God is and "what" God has done. He notes that it is only recently, especially through the contribution of Karl Rahner, that this "formal object" of theology has begun to be redefined so as to embrace communication.

> Classical Thomism, [Rahner] points out, held that the formal object of theology is "God in his godhead" (*Deus sub ratione deitatis*), but this definition was not very helpful in delineating the vital, mysterious, and salvific character of revelation. The classical view, according to Rahner, is acceptable if God is here understood **not** as a self-enclosed Necessary Being—the static object of some kind of natural theology— but precisely in his self-communication.[8]

---

additional chapters. The rest of the text remains unaltered.]. Dulles offers some preliminary remarks regarding symbol and its relationship to revelation and doctrine. These remarks will be explored in depth in the following sections, but it is important to note here that Dulles is moving toward an exploration of the usage of "symbol" and "communication" within the framework of systematic theology. He develops the ideas of "symbolic communication" and "symbolic mediation" in terms of the categories of systematic theology. This link between revelation and communication forms the basis for his position that revelation, because of its inherent quality of, and tendency toward, "symbolic" communication, is foundational for all of theology.

[8]Dulles, *The Craft of Theology,* 21. Our emphasis. Dulles is citing Rahner's article, "Theology, I. Nature," in *Encyclopedia of Theology* (New York: Seabury/Crossroad, 1975), 1686-1695. See *Continued on next page*

Dulles maintains that the "central concern of theology" rests in the exploration of three mysteries inherent in the Christian faith: the Trinity, the Incarnation, and the divinization of human beings. The mystery of the Trinity involves the *inner self-communication* of the divine life and the inner relationships of God's self. The mystery of the Incarnation involves the *self-communication* of the divine λογος in a particular moment in human history in a particular human nature. And the mystery of the divinization of the human person is rooted in the *self-communication* of the Holy Spirit. The critical element in all three mysteries is God's "self-communication."

Dulles is quick to point out that God's communication itself is the issue at hand, and not necessarily the activity of, and the particular elements of, communication between human beings. For that reason he acknowledges that the link between theology and communication is tenuous. (As we shall see later, however, the means by which communication between persons takes place are relevant to his discussion of divine self-expression.). Nevertheless, Dulles insists that communication plays a role in all theological reflection. Moreover, the aspect of

---

also Dulles, "Faith and Revelation," in *Systematic Theology: Roman Catholic Perspectives,* 2 volumes, ed. Francis Schüssler Fiorenza and John P. Galvin (Minneapolis: Fortress Press, 1991), 1:106-108.

communication that proves most significant is the "symbolic" one. He argues that,

> when Rahner's concept of self-communication is linked up with his anthropology and his doctrine of symbol . . . the implications for our subject become evident. God's revelation, if it is to come home to human beings as embodied spirits, must come to expression through tangible, social, and historically transmitted symbols. The divine self-communication, therefore has a social and symbolic dimension.[9]

With his notion of symbolic communication already in place, Dulles asserts that it is not necessary to explore the notion of communication within the framework of fundamental theology ("revelation" being the particular emphasis here) or practical theology (apologetics, missiology, and pastoral theology). In both of these areas, the role of communication is self-evident. Fundamental theology is oriented, though not exclusively, toward God's active *self-communication* to a created reality. Practical theology, in its various dimensions is focused on the human person, the discernment of God's presence in both the community and the individual, as well as the reception and

---

[9]Dulles, *The Craft of Theology*, 22. In the following chapters the anthropologies of Rahner and Dulles will be explored along with their respective definitions of "symbol" and, more specifically, the influence Rahner has had on Dulles' thought.

"translation" of the self-communication of God into a particular framework of life, cultural system, or even into the active spiritual care of the church's members. (Practical theology "cannot be content to establish doctrines by means of formal proof. [It] must be attentive to what is being *communicated* on the subsidiary and even the subliminal level by the Church's whole manner of speaking and acting."[10]) Precisely in order to reflect on how the message of Christ affects both the life of the individual and the life of the community of faith, as well as the corresponding responsibility of a public witness of faith, both fundamental theology and practical theology have long been concerned with the elements of communication. The most significant aspect of Dulles' work is his insistence that it is necessary to begin to explore the significance of communication, specifically, symbolic communication, for systematic theology. In particular, he wants to explore communication in the disciplines of christology, creation, anthropology (grace and sin), ecclesiology, and the Trinity—that is to say, to study the self-communication of God within the context of a total theological system.[11]

Systematic theology has long established that its focal point as a discipline is the "objective reality" of God and the "facts" of salvation history. Dulles notes, however, that while

---

[10]Dulles, *The Craft of Theology*, 25. Our emphasis.
[11]Dulles, *The Craft of Theology,* 26-39.

systematic theologians "have discussed the physical and juridical aspects of sin and redemption, ecclesiology and the sacraments, [they] have not reflected deeply on the nature and efficacy of symbols."[12] He suspects that an espousal of a symbolic dimension of theology, more specifically, symbolic communication's role in theology, may offer new insights and open new paths of dialogue with regard to fundamental and traditional questions of faith and theology.[13] He offers some suggestions as starting points for each of the categories of systematic theology. (The following suggestions are based on his emphasis on both communication and symbol, a theme which will be addressed in detail in the next chapter.)

Christ is the central symbol of the Christian tradition. All Christian theology ultimately refers back to Christ in one fashion or another as its norm, framework, or paradigm. Dulles suspects that within the discipline of *Christology,* this "central symbol" possesses the potential to be developed with reference to the

---

[12]Dulles, *The Craft of Theology,* 26. Our *inclusio.*

[13]In this particular section of *The Craft of Theology*, Dulles begins to speak about "contemporary ecclesial-transformative theology." This category comes from Dulles' reinterpretation of one of the four categories of theology and doctrine explored by George Lindbeck in *The Nature of Doctrine: Religion and Theology in a Postliberal Age* (Philadelphia: Westminster, 1984). An overview of these categories, and this particular "modification" of Dulles, will be explored later on in this chapter and, more extensively, in our chapter four concerning "Dulles and an Ecclesial-Transformative Approach to Revelation."

elements of communication and, most especially, symbol. Classically, the doctrines of Christology focus on the hypostatic union. Dulles suggests that symbolic theology can help "broaden" this doctrine by portraying the incarnation as a mystery of communication. The elements of communication become significant here because, in the incarnation, God "adapts" God's-self within the parameters of human flesh, human history, and human speech. The incarnation is the "self-utterance of God outside himself."[14] As such, the dynamics of communication take on profound proportions.

The discipline of *Creation theology* involves the exploration of the power, nature, and divinity of God as expressed and evidenced (revealed) in the created world. The elements of communication and symbol may offer insight into this discipline in that, as human beings, we are, from the first moment of our existence, oriented toward the divine. Through this orientation, the human being becomes involved in a "dialogue" of discovery, as it were, with the created world and

---

[14]Karl Rahner, "*Zur Theologie der Menschwerdung,*" *Schriften zur Theologie IV,* 137-155, at 149. ["On the Theology of the Incarnation," *Theological Investigations IV: More Recent Writings,* trans. Kevin Smyth (New York: Crossroad, 1966), 105-120, at 115.] *"Die immanente Selbstaussage Gottes in seiner ewigen Fülle ist die Bedingung der Selbstaussage Gottes aus sich weg, und diese setzt jene fort."* Moreover, *"Gottes Logos «wird» Mensch."*

the divine. This dialogue necessitates the involvement of the elements of communication.

> God is at work in the depths of the human psyche, calling it to himself. The discovery of God in nature, like any discovery, depends upon a passionate eagerness to find and on an antecedent conviction that the quest is not in vain. This fiduciary component does not undermine the validity of the discovery, but on the contrary lends assurance that the truth was there, waiting to be found.[15]

The dialogue is, consequently, understood in a metaphorical sense. The dialogue is the very interaction with, and exploration of, nature which ranges from the scientific, in the attempts to "unlock its secrets," to God's revelatory activity in the created world.

Anthropology has assumed greater significance in recent times for the theological enterprise. We today take for granted that the human being is a symbolic animal, one capable of a complex level of communication and possessed of highly-skilled techniques for the engagement with and interpretation of what is

---

[15]Dulles, *The Craft of Theology*, 29. Dulles is citing himself and his considerations of "discovery." See Avery Dulles, "Revelation and Discovery," in *Theology and Discovery: Essays in Honor of Karl Rahner, S.J.,* ed. William J. Kelly, S.J. (Milwaukee: Marquette University Press, 1980), 1-29.

being communicated. The "symbolic" and communicative powers of human beings open up all kinds of possibilities for theology. For example, within Christian anthropological categories, sin can be conceived as an inability to communicate. Dulles even points to the biblical roots of this notion, by noting the pericope of the Tower of Babel (Genesis 11:1-9). A more secular image would portray sin as "static" that is carried across radio or television waves. Nothing is communicated; the self-communication of God is "blocked," as it were, by human sinfulness. Grace, on the other hand, may be seen as a form of successful communication. Grace can be explored within the framework of the invisible, interior gift that is centered on the way we communicate with each other, how we relate to each other. It becomes a "transforming" grace in that, through grace and our openness to that gift, we are oriented once again to each other and to the community.[16]

---

[16]For an excellent exploration of grace and its effects on the spirit, mind and body, see Piet Fransen, *The New Life of Grace*, trans. George DuPont, S.J. (London: Goeffrey Chapman, 1969). Fransen points out that grace is commonly understood to have internal effects on the human person. He maintains that this cannot happen without also affecting the body, in its corporeal form, and the corresponding actions, the moral life, of the human person. See especially, 346-347.

Grace, as it affects the recipient, also affects the dynamics of the interpersonal relationships of the recipient. What is communicated to the person, the essential message of redemption and grace, is meaning. The divine presence communicates to us meaning and gives our personal existence its deepest significance.

Continued on next page

The disciplines of *ecclesiology, sacramentology,* and the theology of *ministry* can also be enriched by an investigation of the dynamics of communication and symbol. The Church is perceived both as institution and community. It expresses itself through word and sacrament—the word involving both the Sacred Scriptures and the Tradition of the Church. All these elements characteristically involve communication. Revelation is not, however, simply the communication of a message. Instead, it is the articulation of a *relationship*—a relationship between God and humanity, between God and the Church. The elements of communication ultimately play a significant role in the clarification and acceptance of the "message," and even more importantly, in the relationship. Moreover, sacraments themselves are symbolic. They possess, inherently, the ability and the opportunity to communicate both verbally and non-verbally. There is, then, in the sacraments, yet another concrete possibility for the articulation of the relationship between God and humanity. The theology of ministry (which dovetails, in some respects, with the discipline of pastoral theology) focuses on the expressive activity of the minister, clearly a symbolic

---

This, in turn, affects how we relate and communicate to each other as well as "communicate" the presence of God active in the lives of human beings. Consequently, these elements, and this position of Fransen, opens up new dimensions and possibilities for the discussion of the impact the elements of communication have on a theology of Grace.

figure through whom Christ speaks and acts.[17] It is the work, so to speak, of the minister to insure that the dialogue between the Church, the community of faith, and God through Christ continues.

The discipline of *eschatology* and the themes of heaven, hell, judgement, and purgatory can be approached from the direction of communication as well. The end time, the experience of heaven and hell, the perception, rationale, and necessity of judgement, and the role of purgatory, may be better illuminated if they are each seen within the framework of *what* is being communicated *about* the relationship between God and humanity. Hell can be considered as a *total deafness* to that which God is communicating. It can be seen as a total distancing of one's self from God and from others. Purgatory could be identified as an "opportunity," so to speak, to remove that which is "blocking" our hearing, creating the deafness, to the self-communication of God. Judgement becomes identified with the communication of, or the manifestation of, who we really are (as beings created in the "image and likeness of God") along with the communication of the expectations of how we were to have lived out our life in that image.

As with our human, physical life, the eschaton involves a social dimension. The placement of heaven and the eschaton within the framework of symbolic communication does not

---

[17]Dulles, *The Craft of Theology,* 34.

eliminate or skew this social component. Rather, the social dimension of the eschaton appears to be drawn out and enhanced. The consideration of heaven becomes, necessarily, contiguous with the consideration of our earthly life. The chasm between heaven and earth appears to be bridged. A more radical "connectedness" can be perceived, a more intimate relationship between the present and the eschaton.

As has been noted above, the *Trinity* is probably the most significant mystery of communication. Dulles maintains that "the Trinity is communication in absolute, unrivaled perfection, a totally free and complete sharing among equals."[18] The divine communication between the three persons of the one God form the framework of this area of theological exploration. The dynamics and elements of the process of communication can serve not only to open up new ways of understanding or expressing the Trinity, but also to clarify the multifarious data contained in the Catholic Christian tradition.

Dulles makes it clear that his point of departure is the conviction that every area of theology is permeated by the theme of divine communication. His emphasis on the dynamic process of communication and his fundamental presupposition concerning "symbolic theology" constitutes a real challenge to the theological enterprise. He believes that Bernhard Häring best summarizes his thesis:

---

[18]Dulles, *The Craft of Theology,* 37.

> Communication is constitutive in the mystery of
> God. Each of the three Divine Persons possesses
> all that is good, all that is true, all that is beautiful,
> but in the modality of communion and
> communication. Creation, redemption, and
> communication arise from this mystery and have
> as their final purpose to draw us, by his very
> communication, into communion with God.
> Creating us in his image and likeness, God makes
> us sharers of his creative and liberating
> communication in communion, through
> communion, and in view of communion.[19]

The preceding reflections were intended to highlight the
relevance of the topic and to set the stage for a recognition that
the theme of revelation is fundamental for all of theology. It is
quite obvious that Dulles frames his position with the idea of
symbolic communication. God's self-disclosure to humanity,
within the course and framework of human history (God's
adaptation, as it were, of God's self to the parameters of history
and, even more specifically, in and through Jesus Christ), is the
ultimate material from which all theological reflection and
discourse flows.

---

[19]Bernhard Häring, *Free and Faithful in Christ*, 2 volumes
(New York: Seabury/Crossroad, 1979), 2:155. Quoted in Dulles, *The
Craft of Theology*, 39.

Before we proceed any further it is necessary to reflect briefly on the categories of George Lindbeck (as Dulles will define himself within this system later on). It may also prove helpful to provide an overview of the classic work of Dulles on revelation; specifically, the five models, in terms of which revelation is most commonly discussed, as found in *Models of Revelation.*

Revelation and George Lindbeck's Categorization of Theories of Doctrine

In 1984, George A. Lindbeck, Pitkin Professor of Historical Theology at Yale University, published a book titled *The Nature of Doctrine: Religion and Theology in a Postliberal Age.*[20] In it he presented a categorization of approaches to doctrine that are, for him, characteristic of the prevailing theories of doctrine. Avery Dulles addresses this categorization of doctrine in *The Craft of Theology*, specifically directing his attention to the way revelation is perceived within each category. He defines his own theological enterprise within (and against) Lindbeck's categorizations. Lindbeck classifies three approaches to doctrine: cognitive-propositionalist, experiential-expressivist, and cognitive-experiential. He also explores a proposed fourth

---

[20]George A. Lindbeck, *The Nature of Doctrine: Religion and Theology in a Postliberal Age* (Philadelphia: Westminster Press, 1984).

category—namely, cultural-linguistic, as shaped by philosophy and the social sciences. For Lindbeck, a new categorization of doctrine is necessary because he considers all the "standard theological approaches [to be] unhelpful."[21] His choice of the word "unhelpful" is influenced by the fact that he perceives a "growing dissatisfaction with the usual ways of thinking about those norms of communal belief and action which are generally spoken of as the doctrines or dogmas of churches."[22]

An Analysis of the Traditional Approaches to Doctrine

The so-called cognitive-propositionalists hold that doctrine functions as "informative propositions or truth claims about objective realities."[23] This approach involves a preoccupation with the "cognitive or informational meaningfulness of religious utterances."[24] For the cognitive-propositionalist, these utterances are divinely given and divinely guaranteed. Hence, revelation is essentially propositional and expresses the objective truth in formulae to which the intellect assents.

---

[21]Lindbeck, *The Nature of Doctrine,* 6.
[22]Lindbeck, *The Nature of Doctrine,* 7.
[23]Lindbeck, *The Nature of Doctrine,* 16.
[24]Lindbeck, *The Nature of Doctrine,* 16. See also, 23, 47, 63-64, 69.

According to Dulles, the Roman Catholic "equivalent" to the cognitive-propositionalist view is found in scholasticism and, more recently, neo-scholasticism. He notes that, for the neo-scholastics,

> revelation is understood as divine doctrine—that is to say, a body of truth that is intended to inform people about the nature of ultimate reality so that they may rightly direct their lives to their last end . . . Revelation [also] gives information about created realities in relation to God, and especially about Christ.[25]

The central kernel of "information" inherent in this doctrine is clearly God—God's self and the mystery of the Trinity.

The experiential-expressive theory of doctrine perceives doctrine to be composed of "noninformative and nondiscursive symbols of inner feelings, attitudes, or existential orientations."[26] The central feature of this category is the recognition that doctrine originates in the interior life and in the personal, subjective (though not necessarily individualistic) experience of the divine. The roots of the experiential-expressive theory can be traced to the work of the German theologian, Friedrich Schleiermacher (1768-1834).

---

[25]Dulles, *The Craft of Theology*, 17. See also Dulles, *Models of Revelation*, 36-52, especially 38, 42-44, 45.
    [26]Lindbeck, *The Nature of Doctrine*, 16. See also, 20, 23, 31-32, 47, 77.

According to Dulles, doctrine, in this category, is held to express "symbols of the inner sentiments of the faithful." Revelation, then, is maintained,

> to consist of privileged inner experiences. The historical and dogmatic contents of faith are of interest only to the extent that they serve to intensify or illuminate present encounters with the divine. Doctrine aims to express and communicate the experience of grace.[27]

Hence, the inner experience of the individual becomes the primary source for whatever is said about the divine or believed to be an encounter with the self-communication of God. According to Lindbeck, this inner experience, in the "prereflective experiential depths of the self," is the basis for all "ultimately significant contact" with that which is finally important to religion (religion understood as an "externalization," publicly and culturally expressed, of just such experiences).[28]

The cognitive-experiential theory of doctrine is, as Lindbeck points out, a hybrid of the cognitive-propositional and experiential-expressive theories. It is "especially favored by ecumenically minded Roman Catholics."[29] In this theory, both

---

[27]Dulles, *The Craft of Theology*, 17-18. See also, 77-78. See also Dulles, *Models of Revelation*, 68-83, 98-114, especially 69, 70-74, 77, 103, 109.

[28]Lindbeck, *The Nature of Doctrine*, 21. See also, 31-32.

[29]Lindbeck, *The Nature of Doctrine*, 16.

elements of religion and doctrine, the "cognitively propositional" and the "expressively symbolic," are seen as appropriate, necessary, and valid. This particular categorization holds, however, no significant import or insight for this inquiry into revelation and symbolic communication. In fact, when Lindbeck's categories are commonly referred to, this one is usually not mentioned. (Lindbeck, himself, "subsumes" it under its component approaches in his own treatment.) It is the "fourth" category, Lindbeck's proposed own "alternative," the "cultural-linguistic" theory, that is listed with the first two. Avery Dulles identifies his own position within the framework of this "alternative" category.

The Cultural-Linguistic Theory of Doctrine

Within the cultural-linguistic approach, doctrine is understood as "communally authoritative rules of discourse, attitude and action."[30] Doctrine offers the guidelines within

---

[30]Lindbeck, *The Nature of Doctrine,* 18. Lindbeck compares this particular theory of doctrine, more specifically, the "religious system" identified from this perspective, to a "cultural-linguistic system." He argues that the characteristics of a "cultural and/or linguistic framework" are much the same as those of a "religious system." "Its doctrines, cosmic stories or myths, and ethical directives are integrally related to the rituals it practices, the sentiments or experiences it evokes, the actions it recommends, and the institutional forms it develops." See *The Nature of Doctrine*, 33. See also, 23, 32-41, 51, 62, 64, 69.

which a particular community of faith lives out its life. It controls and regulates the *way* in which a particular community thinks, speaks, and acts. The language of the community, its history and its communal narratives, hold a significant place in this approach, for they *affect* the patterns of life unique to the community. Dulles views doctrine in this category as "communally authoritative rules of speech and behavior."[31] What is particularly interesting with respect to this category is the notion of community and the necessity of the "interiorization" of the language, the myths and the narrative—that is to say, the doctrine of the community—in order to be religious. One must be a full *participant* in the life of the community for religiosity to be embraced and expressed. For Lindbeck, to be religious,

> is to interiorize a set of skills by practice and training. One learns how to feel, act, and think in conformity with a religious tradition that is, in its inner structure, far richer and more subtle than can be explicitly articulated. The primary knowledge is not *about* the religion, nor *that* the religion teaches such and such, but rather *how* to be religious in such and such ways. Sometimes explicitly formulated statements of beliefs or behavioral norms of a religion may be helpful in the learning process, but by no means always.

---

[31]Dulles, *The Craft of Theology*, 17. See also, 82.

Ritual, prayer, and example are normally much more important.[32]

The individual, consequently, orders and structures his or her life within the particular "interpretive framework" of a particular community of faith. In other words, the individual finds the environment through which he or she is able to come to an experience and understanding of the self-disclosure of the divine. In turn, the individual begins to conform to that "experience" through, and with, the guidance of the community.

For Dulles, because of the social/communal dimension of knowledge and the relationship between the community and the individual, this classification corresponds to the "postcritical

---

[32]Lindbeck, *The Nature of Doctrine*, 35. Lindbeck's emphasis. Lindbeck states elsewhere that religions, understood from this perspective, are to be identified as different "interpretive frameworks" for "constructing reality, expressing experience, and ordering life." See *The Nature of Doctrine,* 47-48. Furthermore Lindbeck notes that the "interpretive framework"—that is to say, the myths, narratives and ritual of a particular tradition—is grounded in the attempt to "articulate or represent and communicate [the] inner experience of the divine." See *The Nature of Doctrine,* 47. See also, 32-33.

See also Avery Dulles, "Faith, Church, and God: Insights from Michael Polanyi," *Theological Studies 45* (1984), 537-550, especially 540-546. Dulles highlights, in this article, some particular themes as "insights" from Polanyi. These insights are not only interesting to Dulles but, ultimately, shape his thought— namely, the notion of "indwelling, that of "conviviality" (which,
Continued on next page

turn"[33] in which theology now finds itself. For Dulles this is not only a significant event but also a necessary and fruitful one. It is

---

as Dulles points out, may well correspond in theological language, to *koinonia)*, and religious worship.

[33]Dulles, *The Craft of Theology*, 15. Earlier in Dulles' first chapter, he explores the movement from the precritical to a postcritical era of theology. He notes that it is "evident" that we are "moving" into realms significantly different than the past centuries. The "postcritical era," more specifically, "postcritical thinking, does not reject criticism but carries it to new lengths, scrutinizing the presuppositions and methods of the critical program itself." Dulles contends that the "critical program" has five flaws. The critical program: [1] "was animated by a bias toward doubt" and held that truth was found in "uprooting all voluntary commitments;" [2] "failed to recognize that doubt itself, and consequently criticism, rests on a fiduciary basis;" [3] is "impossible" to apply consistently; [4] "neglects the social [communal] dimension of knowledge" and "implicitly assumes" that the *individual* has the ability to properly deal with all the "evidence relevant for solving the question at hand;" and [5] "overlooked the *tacit* dimension of knowledge." This fifth "flaw," Dulles maintains, is the most fundamental error. Dulles writes that "even on the most primitive level of visual perception I have to depend on clues that I cannot specify, still less defend, by formal argument. Uninterpreted visual signals, if they may be said to exist at all, are situated at a level below that of explicit awareness. Still more palpably, tacit presuppositions are operative in all human knowledge concerning the facts of history, the findings of science, and the data of religious faith." See *The Craft of Theology*, 5-7. Our *inclusio* and emphasis.

For our purposes, it is important to point out that Dulles recognizes this movement and places himself, the enterprise of theology, and the Church in this "postcritical era." This should be identified as an important presupposition for the development of

Continued on next page

only within the "postcritical" theological enterprise that a renewed exploration of the divine self communication, and symbolic mediation, can find place. Dulles writes that,

> postcritical theology . . . begins with a presupposition of prejudice in favor of faith. Its fundamental attitude is a hermeneutics of trust, not of suspicion. Its purpose is constructive, not destructive . . . But theology, as commonly understood, is the kind of inquiry that takes place from within a *religious commitment.*[34]

Moreover,

> Theology is . . . an ecclesial discipline . . . Theology, then, is a methodical effort to articulate the truth implied in Christian faith, the faith of the Church . . . The method cannot be pursued by the techniques of mathematics or syllogistic logic, but it depends on a kind of *connoisseurship* derived from *personal appropriation* of the *living*

Dulles' thought regarding symbolic communication and revelation, along with Dulles' "redefinition" of Lindbeck's category of "cultural-lingusitic."

See also George A. Lindbeck, "Dulles on Method," in *Pro Ecclesia 1: 1 (1992)*, 53-62, with a rejoinder by Avery Dulles, 61-62. Lindbeck offers a review and a critique of some of the more salient methodological features as found in Dulles' book, *The Craft of Theology.*

[34]Dulles, *The Craft of Theology,* 7. Our emphasis.

faith of the Church. The correct articulation of the meaning of the Christian symbols is not a science learned out of books alone but rather *an art acquired through familiarity by being at home in the community* in which the symbols function. To apprehend the meaning of the symbols, it is not enough to gaze at them in a detached manner as objects and dissect them under a logical microscope. The joint meaning of the symbols cannot be discerned unless one relies confidently on the symbols as clues, and *attends to* the realities to which they point. From within this stance of faith the theologian seeks to formulate in explicit terms what the Christian symbols have to say to the questions that call for solution.[35]

And, finally,

postcritical theology gives new vitality to classical theological loci such as the *"sense of the faithful"* . . . Through *indwelling* in the *community* of faith one acquires a kind of connaturality or connoisseurship that enables one to judge what is or is not consonant with revelation.[36]

---

[35]Dulles, *The Craft of Theology,* 8. Our emphasis.

[36]Dulles, *The Craft of Theology,* 9. Our emphasis. These comments are also an allusion to John Henry Newman's notion of *sensus fidelium,* and to Polanyi's idea of "indwelling." Moreover, the notion of tacit or implicit knowledge, knowledge garnered through "participation in the life of a community of faith," is a pivotal element found throughout the writings of Dulles. See, for example, *The Craft of Theology,* 3-15, especially 6, 9; 17-39,

Continued on next page

Because this "postcritical turn" enables him to significantly rework Lindbeck's category, Dulles renames it "ecclesial-transformative."[37]

The heart of the "ecclesial-transformative" definition, as we shall see in more detail in chapter four, rests in a belief that the locus for understanding the self-communication of God, and its symbolic mediation, is the experience of a community of faith. An "ecclesial-transformative" articulation is intimately tied to "participation," "indwelling," and the "social and communal" dimensions of knowledge. Participation in the community not only assists in the "appropriation" and "apprehension" of the "symbols" that speak of the revelation of God, but also in offering a setting through which the very saving and redeeming communication of God may be experienced. Revelation, then, is to be,

---

especially 19, 20, 24, 25; 53-68, especially 65, 66. See also Dulles, "Faith, Church, and God," 540-542; "Revelation and Discovery," 26-28; *Models of Revelation,* xviii: "All Christian believers, it could be said, tacitly know what revelation is simply by virtue of adherence to a revealed religion. But they do not yet have a formulated concept or theory of revelation." See also Dulles, "From Images to Truth: Newman on Revelation and Faith," *Theological Studies,* 51 (1990), 252-267, especially 260, 261.

See also Thomas Hughson, "Dulles and Aquinas on Revelation," *The Thomist 52* (1988), 445-471.

[37]Dulles, *The Craft of Theology,* 18. See also Marc C. Mattes, review of *The Craft of Theology: From Symbol to System,* by Avery Dulles, S.J., in *Dialog* 34: 2 (Spring, 1995), 144-146.

. . . regarded as a real and efficacious self-communication of God, the transcendent mystery, to the believing community. The deeper insights of revelatory knowledge are imparted, not in the first instance through propositional discourse, but through *participation* in the life and worship of the Church.[38]

But this is to get ahead of ourselves. For the moment, what is important is understanding that Dulles continues to emphasize revelation and its significant role in the broader perspective of theology. Furthermore, his concern for theology and its expression, the role of, and participation in, the community of faith, and the inferred "transformation" of the church on its pilgrim journey throughout the course of human history, are all rooted in his understanding of revelation. At this point it would serve us well to turn to Dulles' own discussion of the models of revelation.

An Overview of Dulles and His Models of Revelation

Models of Revelation, first published in 1983,[39] is one of Dulles' most significant books. In it, Dulles employs his

---

[38]Dulles, *The Craft of Theology,* 18. Our emphasis.
[39]Avery Dulles, *The Models of Revelation* (Maryknoll: Orbis, 1992). The reader is referred to footnote 1.

"trademark" methodology of "models" and sets up a system by which one can explore what revelation is and how it is communicated. Dulles' extensive research, study, and teaching (spanning well over 20 years) in the area of revelation[40] lead him to propose five models of revelation. These are revelation as doctrine, history, inner experience, dialectic presence, and new awareness.

The Propositional or Doctrinal Model of Revelation

The propositional model of revelation holds that revelation is situated primarily in distinct propositional statements attributed to God who is perceived as the authoritative author of these statements. A Protestant characterization of this model sees revelation as identified with the Scriptures which are defined and held to be "inspired and inerrant teachings." The Bible is a "body of objective truth." Within the Roman Catholic perspective, these propositional revelatory statements are characteristically defined by, and identified with, the official teaching of the Church. This teaching is the "body of objective truth."[41]

---

[40]For more indepth coverage on the history of revelation theology, see Avery Dulles, *Revelation Theology: A History* (New York: Herder and Herder, 1969). See also René Latourelle, *Théologie de la révélation* [The Theology of Revelation] (Bruges: Desclée de Brouwer, 1963) [Staten Island: Alba House, 1966].

[41]Dulles, *Models of Revelation,* 27. See also, 36-52.

According to the Roman Catholic view, this truth, formulated with human words, is necessary for salvation because it expresses the salvific activity of God in Jesus Christ—that is to say, it offers us knowledge about God that, consequently, gives us a framework of choice as God's created beings. The moment of revelation is thus located in the formulation and teaching of this truth. It follows, therefore, that the germane response to such revelation is assent, in faith, to such formulation and teaching.

The Historical Model of Revelation

The historical model of revelation takes a position that is in direct opposition to the doctrinal or propositional model. According to this paradigm, God utilizes the course of human history, the history of the created world, to reveal God's presence. "God reveals himself primarily in his great deeds, especially those which form the major themes of biblical history."[42] In contrast to the doctrinal model, here the scriptures and the "official teaching of the church" are considered significant as articulations of revelation only if they distinctly represent God's activity in the created realm. This model addresses the manifestation of "God-in-action," rather than information *about* God stated in propositional form.

---

[42]Dulles, *Models of Revelation,* 27. See also, 53-67.

For those who advocate the historical model, the moment of revelation is found in the occurrence of particular events that give witness to, and offer informed clarity about, God's concern with and plan for, humanity. The pinnacle event within human history, the event that most clearly manifests this "informed clarity," is the Christ event—the life, death and resurrection of Jesus, who henceforth is to be recognized as Lord of all history. Dulles notes that, according to this model, "Hegel was fundamentally correct in maintaining that the meaning of universal history cannot be grasped except from the final outcome. Christian revelation, however, gives us knowledge of the outcome by its anticipation in the fate of Jesus."[43] It follows that the orientation of the human being in light of such "historical" revelation is an enduring and abiding trust, and consequently, hope, in the powerful activity of God's consistent and dynamic interaction, with the world, within human history and in the future of humanity.

The Mystical or Inner Experience Model of Revelation

Revelation as an inner experience is a model that is uniquely juxtaposed to both revelation as doctrine and as history. Revelation as an inner experience is necessarily subjective in character. It is perceived to be a "privileged interior

---

[43]Dulles, *Models of Revelation*, 60.

experience of grace or communion with God,"[44] and thus functions as neither doctrine nor history. The "interior experience" is unmediated and unique to each individual, and the perception of the divine is a matter for the individual him or herself. Some proponents of this model bristle at the individualized character of the "perception of the divine" and, hence, specify the paradigm by maintaining that revelation, in this inner experience, is "contingent" on the mediation of Christ.[45]

The moment of revelation for this model is self-evident. It takes place in the immediate, highly subjective, interior "perception" or awareness of the divine presence. This model identifies the substance—that is to say, the content of revelation—simply as God's loving presence communicated to the individual who stands open before God. It seems clear that the fitting response to this experience of God is to give one's life a specifically "religious" orientation. This orientation is to be understood as living one's life in accord with one's perception of God's expectations but not necessarily in accord with church doctrine or history. In other words, it is a religious "attitude." Having experienced God in such an intimate and personal way, the individual is motivated to orient his or her life toward others and the world, *in the same way* as God has entered into relationship with us.

---

[44]Dulles, *Models of Revelation,* 27. See also, 68-83.

The Dialectical Model of Revelation

Dulles locates the rise of interest in the dialectical model of revelation in the period following World War I, when both the objectivity of the doctrinal and historical models of revelation, and the subjectivity of the inner experience model of revelation frequently were rejected.[46] Those who tend toward this model view God as so utterly transcendent that it is impossible to perceive God from any of the human points of reference elucidated by the other models. It is only through God's encounter with humanity, on God's initiative, through God's word that, because of faith, a person recognizes the presence of God. This "word" of God, which becomes the locus for the encounter, is mediated via the scriptures and the Christian proclamation. In this model, the word of God is in dialectical tension with humanity. The word, spoken and written, provides the media through which the presence of God is made known. This dialectic involves the process of both revealing and concealing the presence of God.

In this model, the moment of revelation finds its place in the dialectic tension that emerges when the word of God is spoken. Consequently the proclamation of God's word is a word "charged with divine power."[47] For the proponents of this

---

[45]Dulles, *Models of Revelation,* 28.
[46]Dulles, *Models of Revelation,* 28. See also, 84-97.
[47]Dulles, *Models of Revelation,* 28.

model, the word is ultimately the "Word" made flesh. Jesus, as the humanly-fashioned Word of God, the divine λογος, is the paradigm for all revelation. The Bible, in and of itself, is not revelation as such, but rather is a reference to, indeed, the primary witness to, the revelation that is Christ, the Word itself. The Church then, understood from the Roman Catholic perspective, to be the living expression of Christ on earth, is, like the Scriptures, only a referent to the Word. The word of the Church, its doctrine and its proclamations, are to be judged according to the supreme point of reference, God's Word, found in the Scriptures. Dulles writes that, "when the Holy Spirit is pleased to speak through the ministry of the church, the preached word and the sacraments become the bearers of revelation."[48] Faith and humble obedience to God are the only proper response. Faith, then, is faith in the Word of God that is at the same time both revelatory and non-disclosive of God. Faith and revelation are inseparable—that is to say, they mutually depend on one another. Nothing is revealed apart from faith.

---

[48]Dulles, *Models of Revelation,* 92.

The New Awareness Model of Revelation[49]

According to the "new awareness" model, revelation "takes place as an expansion of consciousness or shift of perspective when people join in the movements of secular history. God . . . [becomes] not a direct object of experience but is mysteriously present as the transcendent dimension of human engagement in creative tasks."[50] The immanence of God and God's active and creative workings within the context of human

---

[49]It is important to note, that in his 1980 article, "The Symbolic Structure of Revelation," *Theological Studies 41* (1980), 51-73, Dulles uses the term "symbolic model" for what he identifies as "new awareness" in *Models of Revelation.*

In the 1992 preface to *Models of Revelation*, Dulles acknowledges the confusion that surfaced because of this problematic terminology. To be clear, he quickly points out that he is not advocating a "new," "symbolic," model in place of the other five. Rather, he is developing a notion of symbol and symbolic communication, and a doctrine of "symbolic realism," which are to be seen in light of their ability to provide insight and fullness, correction and clarification to the five models. See *Models of Revelation*, viii.

[50]Dulles, *Models of Revelation*, 28. See also, 98-114. Dulles points out that, for the proponents of this model, revelation is an "expansion of consciousness" that takes place when people "join in the movements of secular history." This is not to presume that revelation happens at "any time and place," for "anyone." The key element of this model is situated in the recognition of God's presence through "human engagement in creative tasks." The presumption inherent in this model is an active responsibility of the "believer" for "the concrete actuality of revelation itself . . ." See *Models of Revelation*, 111.

history and the created world constitutes the principal elements of this model. It is *because* of God's immanent presence that men and women can perceive God through their engagement with the created world, their participation in the life of a community of faith, and their utilization of the gifts of creativity and imagination.[51]

For the proponents of the "new awareness" model, the moment of revelation involves the "stimulation of the human imagination" which, in turn, breaks open consciousness, experience, and the whole of the created realm—that is to say, revelation opens up the awareness of new considerations, new avenues of discovery, and new frames of reference, a new awareness of what is "possible." The dynamics of the possible

---

[51]See also Dulles, "Revelation and Discovery," especially 10-13. Dulles quotes a famous passage of Augustine's *Confessions:* "And what is this God? I asked the earth and it answered: 'I am not he,' and all things that are on the earth confessed the same. I asked the sea and the depths and the creeping things with living souls, and they replied: 'We are not your God, look above us.' I asked the blowing breezes, and the universal air with all its inhabitants answered: 'Anaximenes was wrong, I am not god.' I asked the heaven, the sun, the moon, the stars, and 'No,' they said, 'we are not the God for whom you are looking,' And I said to all those things which stand about the gates of my senses: 'Tell me about my God, you who are not He. Tell me something about Him,' And they cried out in a loud voice: 'He made us.' My question was in my contemplation of them and their answer was in their beauty." See Augustine, *Confessions,* Book X, chapter 6, trans. Rex Warner (New York: Mentor-Omega Books, 1963), 215.

take on a new meaning, one that is now situated in the movement of God. Hence, revelation is an on-going, never fully completed process. Because there appears to be no objective truth inherent in this model of revelation, the appropriate response must involve some kind of a deeper personal engagement in one's co-responsibility as co-creator with God through imagination, creative consciousness, and activity in the world. God, to be revealed to us though the "stimulation of the human imagination," characteristically calls one to *use* that imagination within interpersonal and intrapersonal relationships. Revelation, as linked to the "stimulation of the imagination," assists in restructuring experience and, consequently, in transforming one's self and one's world.[52]

Some Concluding Remarks

Dulles maintains that these five models are not exhaustive. They do not, by any stretch of the imagination, cover all the possibilities of the expression and understanding of revelation. (There are also hybrids and nuanced positions, blendings and modifications, as it were, of these five models). He does, however, insist that these are the "principal" systems in the enterprise of revelation

---

[52]Dulles, *Models of Revelation*, 109

The significance of the models of revelation put forth by Dulles will become clear in the following chapters. All these models ultimately rest on recognizing the reality of the divine self-disclosure to human beings. If the content of this revelation is to be meaningful, then what is being disclosed or communicated must fall within the framework of the ability of the human being to understand. This requires that God adapt God's self to the possibilities and limitations of human language—language in its symbolic, social, and interpersonal dimensions. These three dimensions bespeak the major, and most basic, theme of Dulles' enterprise. If God indeed intends for humanity to understand what God communicates within revelation (and it would be senseless to suggest otherwise), than we need to examine how symbolism, social dynamics, and anthropological definitions of the human person can affect, shape, and enhance a theology of revelation. For again, this theology is foundational for every other theological enterprise. Dulles' anthropology, and his understanding of symbol and symbolism, constitutes the subject of the following chapter.

CHAPTER TWO
ANTHROPOLOGICAL CONSIDERATIONS
AND
THE SIGNIFICANCE OF SYMBOL

Anthropology and Symbol

Critical Elements of Anthropology

It is essential to ask basic foundational questions about the human being itself when exploring God's revelation, God's self-communication or self-disclosure, to humanity. What is a human being? What does it mean to be "human?" What are the "characteristics" or, in other words, the elemental factors of humanity? The discipline of anthropology involves not only a survey of these questions but also an inquiry into potential definitions formulated within the framework of particular categories and perceptions. The definitions to be explored in this chapter lie within the particular framework of, and dialogue with, theology—more specifically Christian theology. The interaction

41

between anthropology and theology is critical; the two cannot be separated. Karl Rahner has suggested that while one needs to do anthropology when doing theology, one cannot reduce theology to anthropology.[53] The link between the two can be expressed in the claim that any word spoken about the human being is, at the same time, an insight into God. In other words, language about God is already language about the human being.[54] Definitions,

---

[53]Karl Rahner, "Theologie und Anthropologie," *Schriften zur Theologie VIII,* 43-65, especially 43. ["Theology and Anthropology," *Theological Investigations IX: Writings of 1965-1967,* trans. Graham Harrison (London: Darton, Longman & Todd, 1972), 28-45.] See especially, 28: ". . . [D]ogmatic theology today must be theological anthropology and . . . such an 'anthropocentric' view is necessary and fruitful. The question of man and its answering may not be regarded, therefore, as an area of study separate from other theological areas as to its scope and subject-matter, but as the whole of dogmatic theology itself."

[54]Rahner, "*Theologie und Anthropologie,*" 43. ["Theology and Anthropology," 28.] Rahner writes that, "although anthropocentricity in theology is not the opposite of the strictest theocentricity, it *is* opposed to the idea that . . . it is possible to say something about God theologically without thereby automatically saying something about man and vice versa . . ." Rahner's emphasis.

Rahner sees the human being as utterly incomprehensible apart from God. The question of God's revelation implies the issues of the existence of the human being. See especially Rahner, "*Die theologische Dimension der Frage nach dem Menschen,*" *Schriften zur Theologie XII,* 387-406. ["The Theological Dimension of the Question about Man," *Theological Investigations XVII: Jesus, Man and the Church,* translated by Margaret Kohl (London: Darton, Longman and Todd, 1981), 53-70.]

therefore, about the human being are characterized by a recognition that men and women are created entities of a God who is simultaneously in relationship with those entities.

According to Dulles, specifically Christian anthropology involves a number of important presuppositions. These give rise to a specific definition of the human being. First of all, it needs to be understood that Christian anthropology cannot be explored without reference to Jesus Christ—that is to say, to God made human. The incarnation is central to locating the parameters of the existence of the human being and gaining insight into God and the structure of God's immanence and transcendence. Dulles notes that Vatican II maintained that humanity is revealed to itself in Christ. He quotes from *Gaudium et Spes*: "Only in the mystery of the incarnate Word does the mystery of man take on light." Dulles clarifies this and states that, "theologically speaking, man may be described as what God becomes when God chooses to exist in a nondivine form."[55] The "adaption" of

---

[55]Dulles, *The Craft of Theology,* 30. See *GS* 22. Dulles' clarification is cited as material garnered from Karl Rahner, "Man (Anthropology). III. Theological." *Encyclopedia of Theology*, 887-893, at 893.

See also Rahner, "*Theologie und Anthropologie,*" 43. ["Theology and Anthropology," 28]: ". . . We merely observe that anthropology and Christology mutually determine each other within Christian dogmatics if they are both correctly understood. Christian anthropology is only able to fulfill its whole purpose if it understands man as the *potentia obœdientalis* for the 'Hypostatic Union'. And Christology can only be undertaken from the point of

Continued on next page

the God-self into the categories and limits of the human being opens up incredible possibilities for understanding God's self-communication—in terms of both method and content.

Christian anthropology also involves a process, or movement beyond the scope of one's individual self and one's limited way of viewing reality. Christian anthropology involves more than "me becoming myself." It also focuses on motivating the human being to think in new ways, in new categories, categories that transcend the self and involve the "other" and one's relationship to the "other." Elements of the "relatedness" of God and the relatedness of the human being, intimately linked to the rest of creation, in communion with it, as it were, are found in both the Old and the New Testaments.[56] These elements form the framework through which the human being finds the possibility to come to know God. God cannot exist, *per se,* without human beings. The fundamental expression of God's essence is relationship—God's free, creative and loving activity with humanity.

---

view of this kind of transcendental anthropology . . ." See also Rahner, *"Zur Theologie der Menschwerdung,"* 137-155, especially 141-145. ["On the Theology of the Incarnation," 105-120, especially 109-112.]

[56]For an exploration of one such example of the relational activity of God, specifically in the life of Israel, see Frank Crüsemann, "'You Know the Heart of a Stranger' (Exodus 23:9): A Recollection of the Torah in the Face of New Nationalism and Xenophobia," *Concilium 1993/4, Migrants and Refugees* (New York: Crossroad/Seabury Press, 1993), 95-109.

Christian anthropology also demands an exploration of sin and redemption. Likewise, the distinction and tension between "image and likeness" that has been articulated by theologians (those exploring these notions as related but not identical concepts[57]) must be noted along with a clear representation of how the human being is primarily understood from within these distinctions. Moreover, Christian anthropology requires a fundamental optimism which understands the human person as directed towards God. This "going towards God" flows from a recognition that the human being is the "mirror image of God." The human being, in discovering self (self as *Zustand Möglichkeit*), is discovering God and becoming aware of a responsibility to act as God would be seen to act in Christ Jesus. Since Christian theology always implies anthropology, it is necessary to have a clear definition of the human being as a starting point.

---

[57]See for example, A. G. Hamman, *L'homme, Image de Dieu: Essai d'une anthropologie chrétiene dans l'Eglise des cinq premiers siècles,* Relais-Études 2 (Paris: Desclée, 1987). See also Adolphe Gesché, *Dieu pour penser II: L'homme* (Paris: Cerf, 1993). Today, most, although not all, theologians seem to be in agreement that "image" and "likeness" in the biblical texts mean the same thing.

A Definition of the Human Being

From a Christian point of view, all the characteristics of the human being are evidenced in the life of Jesus, the "perfect" human being—that is to say, the revelation of what a human being is called to be. The human being is perceived, at its very core, to possess the ability to "relate." More precisely, we can say that the human being is in relationship to itself, to others, to God and to the rest of creation. The human being is a "societal" and "communal" being, one that never stands on his or her own. Even from the perspective of its "individuality," the human being is dynamically and radically "connected" to the other. The human being grows toward the fullness of self only in and through its relatedness to the other.[58]

The human being possesses the skills of language, the capacity for thought, and the ability to question. These elements offer an environment in which the human being, in a radical openness to the transcendent, that which is beyond the self, can search for meaning and an understanding of experience. These constitutive characteristics become linked with the God's self-communication—that is, with revelation. Rahner maintains that the human being, him or herself, is the "event of a free, unmerited

---

[58]This is a significant element in the anthropology of Karl Rahner along with his theology of symbol (we shall address this shortly). It becomes a substantial contributing factor in Dulles' own understanding of the human being.

and forgiving, self-communication of God . . . [Moreover], the term 'self-communication' is really intended to signify that God in his own most proper reality makes himself the innermost constitutive element of man."[59] In other words, the relationship expressed is not God *and* the human being but God *in* the human being.

The human being is a unified being—that is to say, an embodiment of wholeness, freedom and responsibility. The human being is also a historical being, one that is conditioned and characterized by space, time (the past, the present, and the "potential" of the future), and environment. From the Christian perspective, then, the human being becomes historically linked, as sinner and as one redeemed, to God and the rest of creation through the Fall, and the incarnation and resurrection of Jesus.

In a 1980 article, "The Symbolic Structure of Revelation," Dulles writes that, for many contemporary thinkers,

---

[59]Karl Rahner, *Foundations of Christian Faith: An Introduction to the Idea of Christianity* (New York: Crossroad, 1989), 116. Our *inclusio*. Rahner points out that he is dealing with an *"ontological"* self-communication of God. See also, 117-126.

See also Dulles, "Revelation and Discovery," 10-11. Dulles contends that "the religious quest . . . begins with passionate questioning." Moreover, "the religious inquirer is existentially involved in the search, for the questions are of ultimate concern to the subject as person." Furthermore, "if we take our eyes off the God for whom we are looking the whole quest collapses."

to be human . . . is to be a body-person, an incarnate spirit. To come into one's own as a person is, under one aspect, to become related, through the body, to a surrounding world. Religious awareness [understood as relatedness to God and an awareness of one's freedom and responsibility], paradoxically, requires a turning *to* the world; for only in a spiritual movement toward finite realities can one actuate the sense of the transcendent as that which goes *beyond* the world.[60]

More recently, with the publication of *The Craft of Theology* in 1992, Dulles clarifies this definition within his own perspective and with his own terms. He offers a definition of the human being that proves critical for his exploration of the symbolic self-communication of God. Dulles writes that,

to be human is to be *socially and historically* constituted. As social beings, human persons realize themselves through bodily *communication*

---

[60]Dulles, "The Symbolic Structure of Revelation," 59-60. Our *inclusio*. See Dulles, *The Assurance of Things Hoped For: A Theology of Christian Faith* (New York: Oxford University Press, 1994), 217. Here Dulles cites Ian G. Barbour and his proposition of "seven common forms of religious experience: Awe and reverence, Mystical union, Moral obligation, Reorientation and reconciliation, Interpersonal relationships, Key historical events, and Order and creativity in the world," as found in: Ian G. Barbour, *Myths, Models and Paradigms* (New York: Harper & Row, 1974), 53-56.

[including language], which is symbolic insofar as
the bodily gestures and actions [and words],
manifest the ideas and ideals of individuals in
community. As historical beings, men and women
achieve the benefits of culture by appropriating
the insights of their forebears, as these insights are
transmitted in the cultural heritage. The
assimilation of social and historical symbols
requires readiness *to open oneself* to the ideas and
values that these symbols embody. [61]

Because Dulles situates the human being in a symbolically
defined context, it is necessary to carefully define "symbol" as

---

[61]Dulles, *The Craft of Theology*, 20-21. Our *inclusio* and
emphasis. This perspective on the human being is held within the
context of Rahner's ontology of symbol and his theological
anthropology. "The human person, it is held, consists of a spirit
that realizes itself in the body to which it is dialectically united.
The body is, so to speak, the self as other. It is not a mere
appendage of a spirit that has its own existence, but is the self-
expression of the spirit in a form other than its own. The two-in-
oneness of body and spirit characterizes the whole of human life."
See *The Craft of Theology,* 20. Dulles goes on to say (p.21) that,
"the same principles apply to religion, which is an instance of
social and historical existence. Christian symbols call for openness;
they both demand and make possible a radical change in the
hearers' attitudes and behavior. Thus revelation and redemption are
two aspects of the same coin. Faith is not just an act of the
intellect but a transformation of the whole person in response to
God's initiatives, conveyed through the religious community and its
tradition."

Dulles uses the term—a term that identifies the central element in his theological enterprise.

The Significance of Symbol and Symbolism

Dulles initiates the exploration of his understanding of symbol and symbolic language[62] by weaving together the strands

---

[62]As we enter more deeply into the theology of symbol held by Avery Dulles, it will be necessary to recognize and understand the formidable influence of Karl Rahner and his theology of symbol. Throughout this section, consequently, we will make occasional reference to the work of Rahner as it pertains to Dulles.

From the outset, however, it must be clear what the "task" of Rahner is for his theology of symbol. This "task," which clearly delineates his theology as "symbolic," is to ". . . look for the highest and most primordial manner in which one reality can represent another—considering the matter primarily from the formal ontological point of view. And we call this supreme and primal representation, in which one reality renders another present (primarily 'for itself'[*«für sich»*] and only secondarily for others), a symbol: the representation which allows the other 'to be there [*«da-sein»*]'." See Rahner, *"Zur Theologie des Symbols," Schriften zur Theologie, Band IV,* 275-311, at 279. ["The Theology of the Symbol," *Theological Investigations IV: More Recent Writings,* translated by Kevin Smyth (London: Darton, Longman and Todd, 1959), 221-252, at 225.]

Moreover, the ontology of symbolization that Rahner develops is formulated in terms of three key axioms. They are, namely, the unity and multiplicity of Being, *Selbstvollzug* and *Selbstausdruck*, and Being as *Beisichsein,* and they ". . . point to the need for all beings to be symbolic in the primary sense (*Realsymbole*) and - in turn - allow them to be symbolic in the

Continued on next page

secondary sense (*Vertretungssymbole*)." See Albert Liberatore, "Symbols in Rahner: A Note on Translation," *Louvain Studies 18* (1993), 151-155.

To clarify these Rahnerian terms, Liberatore points out that "to the secondary, derived symbols he [Rahner] assigns the term *Vertretungssymbole*, which he uses as a general heading for arbitrary 'signs' (*Zeichen*), 'signals' (*Signale*), and 'codes' (*Chiffren*). For 'primary' or 'original' symbols, on the other hand, he uses the term *Realsymbole*, which he defines as 'the self-realization of a being in the other, which is constitutive of its essence.' The criterion for determining whether or not a given symbol is a *Realsymbol*, then, is the intrinsicity of the relationship between the two beings (i.e., whether or not the symbol is the expression of the other being, for that being's self-realization). If it is, then the symbol in question is a *Realsymbol*; if it is not, then the symbol in question is a *Vertretungssymbol*; and, in either case, it is still rightly called a symbol." See "Symbols in Rahner," 148.

Rahner maintains that "every being as such possesses a plurality as intrinsic element of its significant unity; this plurality constitutes itself, by virtue of its origin from an original unity, as the way to fulfill the unity (or on account of the unity already perfect), in such a way that that which is originated and different is in agreement with its origin and hence has (as least in a 'specificative', if not always in a 'reduplicative' sense) the character of expression or 'symbol' with regard to its origin . . . [Therefore] being is of itself symbolic, because it necessarily 'expresses' itself." See *"Zur Theologie des Symbols,"* 283-284. ["The Theology of the Symbol," 229, 225-226.] This understanding manifests itself in the thought of Dulles in his claim that the "plenitude of meaning" present in a symbol is "evoked" and not explicitly stated. See, for example, Dulles, "The Symbolic Structure of Revelation," 62-68, especially 66; *Models of Revelation*, 132; *The Craft of Theology*, 20, 22-39, 65. This will become more clear as we explore the actual characteristics of symbol and symbolic language for Dulles.

Continued on next page

of elements found in both secular and religious literature.[63] In so doing, he lays the groundwork for articulating the inherent characteristics of symbol and symbolic language. His aim, ultimately, is to create a framework for the analogy he develops with the significant elements of the event of revelation.

Dulles begins by pointing out that a "symbol is a special type of sign [that needs] to be distinguished from a mere indicator (such as the shadow on a sun dial) or a conventional cipher (such as a word or diagram). A symbol is a sign pregnant with a plenitude of meaning which is evoked rather than explicitly stated."[64] One sphere of human life in which symbols

---

Rahner holds that "a being is also 'symbolic' in itself because the harmonious expression, which it retains while constituting it as the 'other,' is the way in which it communicates itself to itself in knowledge and love. A being comes to itself by means of 'expression,' in so far as it comes to itself at all. The expression, that is, the 'symbol'—as the word is now to be understood in the light of the foregoing considerations—is the way of knowledge of self, possession of self, in general." And, consequently, ". . . the symbol is the reality in which *another* attains knowledge of a being." See *"Zur Theologie des Symbols,"* 285. ["The Theology of the Symbol," 230.] Rahner's emphasis.

[63]Dulles, for his purposes in this exploration, simply understands religious literature, as opposed to secular literature, to be that of the Sacred Scriptures and other "religious writings" that, from a perspective of faith, deal with the self-revelation of the divine.

[64]Dulles, *Models of Revelation*, 132. Dulles makes his readers aware that his understanding of symbol and, ultimately, his definition, is similar to what Philip Wheelwright calls "tensive

Continued on next page

are commonly perceived and spoken of is the world of Fine Arts. Here, specifically, our example will be literature. Inherent in the

---

symbols." These "tensive symbols" stand, for Wheelwright, in contrast to "steno-symbols." "Tensive symbols" are seen as symbols which "'draw life from a multiplicity of association, subtly and for the most part subconsciously interrelated,' and which thereby derive the power to tap a vast potential of semantic energy." Cf. [P]. H. Wheelwright, *Metaphor and Reality*, (Bloomington: Indiana University Press, 1962), 94. Wheelwright goes on to point out that "Steno-symbols" possess an "exact identity of reference" and are perceived to be what most people understand as "signs." Cf. Dulles, "The Symbolic Structure of Revelation," 56-57.

Dulles also points out that Michael Polanyi makes a similar distinction yet utilizes different terminology in its expression. Polanyi speaks of symbol and indicators. Indicators, indicative signs, are held to be, as the name suggests, those factors that function in a "purely subsidiary way, so that without being attended to they direct our attention to other objects which are focally known. When, for example, we read a letter, we hardly notice the print or even the language, since our attention is directed to the meaning. The indicative signs lack intrinsic interest. We interpret them as mere observers, without being deeply moved by the signs themselves." See *Models of Revelation*, 132. See Michael Polanyi and H. Prosch, *Meaning* (Chicago: University of Chicago Press, 1975), 69-75.

See also Kelly, "Knowing by Heart," 68: "Real symbols differ from merely representative or empty signs by *being* the very presence of the reality they signify." Kelly's emphasis.

Dulles, comparing his ideas to Rahner's, points out that his [Dulles'] term "'*presentative symbol*' corresponds approximately to what Rahner has called 'symbolic reality' (*Realsymbol*) as distinct from 'symbolic representation' (*Vertretungssymbol*)." See Dulles, "The Symbolic Structure of Revelation," 68, n. 44.

usage of symbol in fine literature is a perceived intimate relationship between the symbol, as such, and the multitude of literary styles and devices such as analogy, myth, metaphor, allegory, and parable. Religious literature—that is to say, writings that are seen to be "codifications" of "divine revelation"—employs both symbol and these literary devices in rich and demanding ways. Dulles cautions that, when revelation is at issue, the notion of symbol cannot, and must not, remain solely in the realm of literary symbolization. This is only a starting point, a locus of understanding and initial clarity, since the notion of symbol is much broader than the literary sense of the term. To restrict the utility of symbol to one particular venue is to limit the very nature of symbol itself. Dulles makes it clear that "natural objects, historical persons, visible artifacts, and dreams can all be symbols. [And], in the sphere of religion, it is helpful to distinguish between cosmic or natural symbols (such as the sun), personal or historical symbols (such as David and the Davidic monarchy), and artistic symbols (such as temples and icons)."[65]

Symbolic language, the *articulation* of some dimension of reality through the use of the symbol, gives rise to the expression of something that is beyond the expressive ability of normal discourse. Revelation, the self-communication of God, is understood as something that goes beyond, or transcends normal

---

[65]Dulles, *Models of Revelation*, 133.

human discourse and can, therefore, be illuminated by the category of symbol. Dulles is aware that,

> in speaking of revelation as symbolic disclosure, theologians are generally using 'symbol' in an inclusive sense that would include not only visible or tangible objects [or persons] but also the 'charged' language of more-than-literal speech.[66]

But to speak of revelation as symbolic disclosure, and to understand the corresponding use of symbol in this "inclusive" sense, it must be fundamentally clear what one means by "symbol" and "symbolic language."

Can the symbol function in a "revelatory" fashion? What are its characteristics, its internal dynamics, so that it can serve as an expression of something "more-than-it-is," of the being of another, of the self-disclosure of the divine? From where does it derive its power of expression? These are the questions to which we must now turn our attention.

---

[66]Dulles, "Symbolic Structure of Revelation," 56-57. Our *inclusio*. In another place Dulles maintains that "a revelation that begins with symbolic communication gradually generates a whole series of reflections and interpretations that explicate its meaning." See Dulles, "Faith and Revelation," 97.

The Nature of Symbol

Dulles' goal is to provide confirmation that revelation, by its very nature, is symbolic. His attempt to ferret out and identify the unique characteristics of symbol and symbolism is informed by the conviction that such information can, in turn, provide the elements for setting up a "parallelism between the properties of symbolic communication and revelation."[67] This "parallelism" becomes the argument by which he is able to offer confirmation for his propositions regarding the symbolic nature of revelation.

Dulles maintains that symbol and symbolism have four properties.[68] These are, first, the ability of symbol and

---

[67]Dulles, *Models of Revelation*, 136.

[68]Dulles, *Models of Revelation,* 136. Cf. Dulles, "The Symbolic Structure of Revelation," 59-65. Dulles observes, in a footnote, that "the three properties of symbol discussed in the following paragraphs may be compared with the six examined by M. Eliade in his "Methodological Remarks on the Study of Religious Symbolism," in *The History of Religions,* ed. M. Eliade and J. M. Kitagawa (Chicago: University of Chicago Press, 1959), 98-103.

"According to Eliade, religious symbols (1) disclose modalities of the real not evident in ordinary experience, (2) refer to real structures of the world, (3) are multivalent, (4) reveal perspectives in which heterogeneous realities can be articulated into a whole, (5) make it possible to express paradoxical situations otherwise inexpressible, and (6) addresses situations in which human existence is engaged." This is Dulles' formulation as found in *Models of Revelation,* 306, n. 16.

Continued on next page

symbolism to offer "participatory knowledge;" second, their "transforming effects"—that is to say, their ability to engage the person on the level of the human psyche which can effect "change" in the person; third, their "influence on commitments, behaviors and actions" of the human being; and, fourth, their ability to open up "new avenues of awareness" and insight. We will examine each of these properties separately.

Participatory Knowledge

Symbolism offers "not speculative knowledge but participatory knowledge— knowledge, that is to say, of a self-involving type."[69] Dulles explains that this "self-involving knowledge" makes a symbol function not as an object but as a "lure" which draws the human being into "participation" in its multifarious milieu of meaning. He clarifies this idea of

It is important to point out that, in "The Symbolic Structure of Revelation" (1980), Dulles held only "three properties;" the property of "participatory knowledge" was conjoined with revelation's "transformative effects." Dulles maintained that "participatory knowledge" is what provokes the "transforming effects" on the person. By the time *Models of Revelation* was published in 1983 (the article was reworked to become "Chapter 9"), however, Dulles had "split," as it were, these two elements. Yet, there was no correction to the text, and the footnote in *Models of Revelation* continues to speak of "three."

[69]Dulles, *Models of Revelation,* 136. See also Dulles, *The Craft of Theology,* 65: "A symbol . . . communicates by inviting people to *participate* in its own meaning . . ."

"participatory knowledge" by quoting Nathan Mitchell, who maintains that a symbol is ". . . [a] place to live, . . . an environment to be inhabited."[70]

Symbols, therefore, are elements to be engaged and places of "discovery."[71] To understand the dynamics of "participatory knowledge," one may think of a Museum of Fine Arts, for example. An art museum is a place that contains a collection of works of art from many different artists, of many different styles, periods of time and influence, and mediums of execution. A person may simply walk through the museum and categorize, enumerate, and distinguish the elemental factors inherent in the collection. Or a person may walk through the museum "attending from"[72] the works of art as the "symbolization" of something

---

[70]Nathan Mitchell, "Symbols are Actions, Not Objects," *Living Worship 13/2* (February, 1977), 1-2.

[71]See Dulles, "Revelation and Discovery," 4, 5, 19-24, 27.

[72]It would appear at first glance that the phrase should read "'attending to' the works of art . . ." This particular formulation of words, "attending from" something and "attending to" something, is based on the work of Michael Polanyi, *The Tacit Dimension* (Garden City: Doubleday Anchor Books, 1967), 4, 8, 15-16, 18. Polanyi's epistemology involves the concept of "indwelling" or "attending"—that is to say, the "personal participation of the knower in what he or she knows." Polanyi maintains that we know something not by "attending to" the object (which would imply an objective acknowledgment of the object) but by "attending from" or "dwelling in" it (which involves an intimate relationship with the object at hand). Polanyi uses the example of the body. We "know" our body through "participation" ("attending from") in it and not simply by looking at it as if in a mirror ("attending to").

Continued on next page

beyond the particular canvas or clay, or whatever medium, and be "lured" into the more—that is to say, participate in the work of art itself, in the life of the artist, in the multiplicity of meaning captured in the inks, the paints, the clay. By "participation" in the work of art, the "symbol," as it were, new discoveries, new knowledge and insights and awareness come as "gift" to the beholder.

Transformative Effects

"Symbol, insofar as it involves the knower as a person, has a transforming·effect."[73] In asserting this characteristic of symbol, Dulles is concretely aware of the "power," so to speak, that the inherent meanings of a symbol have over the psyche of a human being. Phrases expressive of this power include: "I was really 'moved' by that work of art." "We were 'touched' by the

---

This notion of "indwelling," "attending from," is correlative to the first characteristic of symbol, "participatory knowledge." See also Polanyi, "Faith and Reason," *Journal of Religion 41* (1961), 237-247, especially 239, 241-242.

[73]Dulles, *Models of Revelation*, 136. See Dulles, "Revelation and Discovery," 4: "Discovery [through symbol] is an insight that *changes* the knower's outlook and horizons." Our *inclusio* and emphasis. See also Dulles, *The Craft of Theology,* 22-24, at 22: ". . . These signs both call for, and have the power to affect conversion." Moreover, "symbols do something to us . . . [They] have a kind of transformative power that is needed for conversion to come about." See *The Craft of Theology*, 65.

generosity of your action." "The singing of our National Anthem and seeing our country's flag flown during the ceremonies 'did something' to us!" Although simple, common, and ordinary, these statements reflect the "transforming" power and polyvalent dynamics of symbol and symbolism as people attempt to articulate the "transformation" that takes place within them after a profound experience of "attending from" particular symbols.

Influence on Commitments and Behaviors

As a consequence of the transforming nature of symbol, Dulles asserts that "symbolism has a powerful influence on commitments and behaviors."[74] He goes on to say that a symbol plays an important role, in that "it stirs the imagination, releases hidden energies in the soul, gives strength and stability to the personality, [and] arouses the will to consistent and committed action."[75] This influence on the commitments, behavior, and motivations of human beings is even more significant than the

---

[74]Dulles, *Models of Revelation,* 137.

[75]Dulles, *Models of Revelation,* 137. See also Dulles, "Revelation and Discovery," 12: "Even after the discovery is made, however, the process of confirmation [the fourth "step" in the process of religious discovery and conversion] goes on . . . Those who have been themselves converted are driven by a passion to convert others, partly in order to share the riches they have found, but partly also to reinforce their own conviction."

transforming effect of symbol, for it alerts us to the social dimensions and implications of symbolism and symbolic communication. A symbol is not something that merely affects the individual him/herself, but rather is something that affects the individual in his or her relationship to others and to his or her surroundings. If this element holds true as a characteristic of the symbolic dimension of revelation (and we shall approach this topic in the next chapter), it has serious ramifications for understanding God's self disclosure. Dulles highlights this characteristic by pointing out that such influence is the reason that social and political movements recognize the need to utilize appropriate symbols for their cause.[76]

New Realms of Awareness

The fourth characteristic of symbol articulated by Dulles is the fact that "symbol introduces us into realms of awareness not normally accessible to discursive thought."[77] Because of the multivalent character of symbols and symbolic language, the symbol possesses the ability to transcend the objective and the empirical world and carry anyone who engages with the symbol

---

[76]Dulles, *Models of Revelation,* 137.

[77]Dulles, *Models of Revelation,* 137. See Dulles, "Revelation and Discovery," 5. Dulles, in articulating the "second stage" in the process of discovery contends that it is a ". . . mysterious stage in which ideas hatch without our being able to control them." See also Dulles, *The Craft of Theology,* 18.

to deeper levels of awareness—awareness with new dimensions and new possibilities. Symbol opens the world of the possible and "gives rise to thought."[78] One can distinguish two dimensions here: first, the "creation" of ideas, and second, the awareness of "higher," "elevated," or "transcendent" ideas. Dulles clarifies this final characteristic of symbol by an appeal to Paul Tillich who recognizes a symbol as that which "opens up levels of reality which otherwise are closed to us . . . and also unlocks dimensions and elements of our soul which correspond to the dimensions and elements of reality."[79]

These four components of symbol—its offer of participatory knowledge, its transformative effects, its consequent influence on commitments and behaviors, and its ability to bring one into new realms of awareness—create an environment within which anyone engaging with the symbol can

---

[78]Paul Ricœur, *Symbolism of Evil* (Boston: Beacon, 1969), 348. This has become a classical formulation. See also Ricœur, *"Herméneutique de l'idée de Révélation,"* in *La révélation,* ed. Paul Ricœur, Emmanuel Levinas, Edgar Haulotte, Etienne Cornélis, and Claude Geffré (Bruxelles: Facultés universitaires Saint-Louis, 1984), 15-54 at 45: *"Mais la réflexion n'est jamais première, jamais constituante: elle survient comme une « crise » au sein d'une expérience qui nous porte et nous constitue proprement en sujet de cette expérience."*

[79]Dulles, *Models of Revelation*, 136-137. Cf. Dulles, "The Symbolic Structure of Revelation," 62. Dulles cites from Paul Tillich, *Dynamics of Faith* (New York: Harper, 1957), 42. See also Dulles, "Revelation and Discovery," 4-10.

"know [infinitely] more than [he or she] can say."[80] Dulles offers yet another point of clarification.

> In symbolic communication, the clues draw attention to themselves. We *attend to* them, and if we surrender to their power they carry us away, enabling us to integrate a wider range of impressions, memories, and affections than merely indicative signs could enable us to integrate.[81]

It is not difficult to understand why Dulles suggests that "these four qualities of symbolic knowledge make it apparent how symbol can be uniquely apt as a medium of revelation; for the

---

[80]This is a formulation found in the epistemology of Michael Polanyi. Polanyi formulates the general principle: "Tacit knowing is more fundamental than explicit knowing: we can know more than we can tell and we can tell nothing without relying on our awareness of things we may not be able to tell." See Polanyi, *Personal Knowledge: Towards a Post-Critical Philosophy* (New York: Harper Torchbooks, 1964), x [Torchbooks Edition Preface]. See also Dulles, "Revelation and Discovery," 9: "The discovery, when it appears, corresponds to what, in the search, we already felt must be there." See also Dulles, *A Church to Believe in,* 42-43, 48.

[81]Dulles, *Models of Revelation*, 132. It would appear that Dulles regards as synonymous much of the specific language utilized by Polanyi. Dulles seems to, first, equate "attending to" something and "attending from" something, thereby making "attending to" synonymous with the notion of "indwelling" or "dwelling in." See Polanyi, *The Tacit Dimension*, 4, 8; *Personal Knowledge*, x, 53-54, 207-209. See also Dulles, *The Craft of Theology*, 8, 9, 24.

qualities of revelation correspond, on a transcendent level, to those just noted in symbolic communication."[82] Nonetheless there are intrinsic nuances to these characteristics when they are at work within the framework of revelation. Within this framework, these specific elements are all essentially influenced by the underlying principle of grace.[83] Put simply, it is because of grace that symbol and revelation become correlative. Dulles points out that,

> . . . the symbol itself, in its full dimensions, includes the experience of grace; for this experience provides the horizon necessary for any external symbol to be discerned as a divine communication. On the other hand, the experience

---

[82]Dulles, *Models of Revelation,* 138. Cf. Dulles, "The Symbolic Structure of Revelation," 63. By "transcendent level" Dulles is referring to the plane of reality where revelation is situated and finds its structure. On this level there is a significant similarity between the "structure" and effect of revelation and the qualities of symbolic knowledge.

[83]Most simply understood, Dulles maintains that the dynamic aspect of grace must be spoken of in terms of internal and external grace. In virtue of Christ's redemption grace has an internal and external influence on the individual, an influence that stems from the seed of "immortality" and "reconciliation." Moreover, "grace . . . has an influence on the way individuals relate to one another." See Dulles, *The Craft of Theology,* 32. For some examples of influences on the thought of Dulles, see Fransen, *The New Life of Grace;* See also Rahner, "*Theologie und Anthropologie,*" 43-65. ["Theology and Anthropology," 28-45.]

of grace cannot be rightly interpreted, or recognized for what it is, without the help of symbols derived from the world known through sensory experience.[84]

The Symbolic Structure of Reality within the Context of Anthropology

According to Dulles, reality has a symbolic structure. The sources of his view in this regard are his own anthropology coupled with the ontology of symbol articulated by Karl Rahner. Dulles holds that the human beings are social creatures who come to an awareness and realization of self through communication,

---

[84]Dulles, *Models of Revelation*, 149: "In Rahnerian terminology, transcendental revelation and categorical revelation are not two separable entities but two dimensions of a single, complex reality [Rahner, *Foundations of Christian Faith*, 171]. Like form and matter, like soul and body, they are mutually dependent and mutually causative; they exist only in their coalescence. *Causae ad invicem sunt causae.*"

Dulles notes that "authors such as Rahner, in their theology of revelation, speak paradoxically of 'mediated immediacy'." It is a "term" that points to the dualism in any revelatory experience. Moreover, "what is immediate, for Rahner, is the self-communication of the divine, the experience of grace [transcendental revelation]. But the inner presence of God cannot be known and cannot achieve itself except insofar as it becomes mediated, or mediates itself, in created symbols [categorical revelation]." See *Models of Revelation,* 148-149. Our *inclusiones.*

See also Dulles, "The Symbolic Structure of Revelation," 69-70.

an activity which is itself symbolic. Human beings are symbolic in their very nature. Dulles agrees with Rahner that "all beings are by their nature symbolic, because they necessarily 'express' themselves in order to attain their own nature."[85] Moreover "the symbol strictly speaking (symbolic reality) is the self-realization of a being in the other, which is constitutive of its essence."[86]

Dulles clarifies this "ontology of symbol" within his own anthropological framework (which also reflects Rahner's influence). Starting with the definition of symbol set forth by Rahner, Dulles is able to formulate an understanding of symbol and symbolic that is determinative of his approach to both the human person and reality as such. Dulles writes:

> The human person, it is held, consists of a spirit that realizes itself in the body to which it is dialectically united. The body is, so to speak, the self as other. It is not a mere appendage of a spirit that has its own existence, but is the self-expression of the spirit in a form other than its own. The two-in-oneness of body and spirit characterizes the whole of human life. The human

---

[85]Rahner, "*Zur Theologie des Symbols,*" 278. ["The Theology of the Symbol," 224.]

[86]Rahner, "*Zur Theologie des Symbols,* 290. ["The Theology of the Symbol," 234.] In an interview with Avery Dulles, Fall 1992, Dulles emphasized the significant influence of Rahner's theory of symbol on his work. He pointed out that the work of Paul Tillich was also an influence but that this was peripheral.

spirit achieves selfhood and maturity not by withdrawal from the body but by developing its thoughts, attitudes, and commitments through the body.[87]

The contextual reality in which a human being experiences the world is itself an essentially symbolic order. This is because symbols (the symbolic) constitute the environment *through* which a human being experiences and moves toward self-realization. Moreover, the symbols that form the environment, and that characterize the expression of the human being possess a paradoxical quality. As Justin Kelly states, in his article reflecting on the work of Dulles:

> Real symbols thus involve a paradoxical presence-in-absence, an identity and a difference. A person's deeds, for instance are a real symbol of the person. I am in my words and action. They are not just external signs of me (like a black, curving arrow on a sign announcing a coming bend in the road), but literally *me*. I exist in them and by means of them. And yet in another way they are not me, but something I do. I exist at other times apart from these particular signs through which I reveal myself now; it may even be that my words and gestures are misleading, deceitful, seeming to show what is not really there.[88]

---

[87]Dulles, *The Craft of Theology*, 20.
[88]Kelly, "Knowing by Heart," 68-69.

Nevertheless this self-realization remains the "self-realization of a being in the other." Participation in the environment of the symbolic, in the symbolic itself (the language, gestures, ideas, the "other"), enables us to communicate who we are and, at the same time, know ourselves.

Communication and Language as Integral to the Human Being

Language and communication are two significant elements of Dulles' anthropology that help him define reality as possessing a symbolic structure. These elements are inherently connected in that human beings communicate through language. Formally understood, language is a systematic means of communicating thoughts, feelings, and ideas by way of words, sounds, gestures, and actions. It involves not only the linguistic representation of that which is to be communicated, but also the "symbols" that give rise to thought and the thought process itself. In turn, communication is the act of transmission of information, in and through language, or the *process* by which information is disseminated from one person to another.

In communication there are three major elements: the *sender or author,* the *receiver* or *recipient,* and the *message* or *content.* The *medium of* communication, the way in which the information is *mediated,* is multifarious. Certain of these media are less effective, and less successful, in assuring clear, articulate, and well-"transmitted" information than others. There are also innumerable external factors that can affect, more often than not with deleterious effects, the transmission of the information. Moreover, external factors or forces can influence both the effectiveness and articulateness of the sender, and the capacity of the receiver to comprehend what is being transmitted.

Within the framework of a theory of revelation, God functions as the sender or *revealer*, while human beings are the *recipients* of what is being revealed—the *content* or the *message* of the revelation. Although external factors can affect the sender's effectiveness within the context of human communication, this cannot be the case within the framework of divine revelation. There is, however, an external factor which predisposes the act of communication by the divine to a particular paradigm—namely, the language and the capacity for (divinely revealed) knowledge of the human being. God must frame the act of self-communication within the parameters of the human condition in order for communication to be successful. In other words, God is dependent on the human condition for the act of self-disclosure, for "God cannot manifest Himself to us except by making signs that are perceptible in the created order."[89] How else could the act of communication be completed, or the message, so to speak, be understood?

---

[89]Dulles, "The Symbolic Structure of Revelation," 60. Charles Davis addresses this same material and cites the constitutive elements of verbal communication as analogous to revelation. He

Continued on next page

A multitude of factors need to be present *in* the receiver, the human being, for revelation to be possible. Two factors are uniquely important for this discussion, namely, language and the ability to know. The human being needs to be an intelligent being, with the ability to communicate him- or herself to other human beings, for the act of revelation of the divine to have any grounding at all. Within the Christian anthropological framework, these elements are already gifts, as it were, from the divine, who desires to communicate with creation—specifically human creation. There is, then, a significant structural relationship involved in the act of communication and the act of revelation.

Nevertheless, there is no guarantee that revelation will be received. As we have already seen in our discussions of Christian anthropology, the human being inevitably is involved in the

---

states that, "since revelation is conceived by an analogy with verbal communication, we may make use here of Roman Jakobson's distinction of the six constitutive factors in any verbal communication. An *addresser* sends a *message* to an *addressee*. To be operative the *message* must be in a *context* and expressed in a common *code*. Finally, there must be some connection or *contact* between the *addresser* and addressee, enabling them to enter and remain in communication. Notice that the meaning is not limited to the *message*, but belongs to the totality of the verbal communication with its six constituent factors." See Charles Davis, *Religion and the Making of Society: Essays in Social Theology* (Cambridge: Cambridge University Press, 1994), 98. Here he cites two texts of Roman Jacobson as found in David Lodge, ed., *Modern Criticism and Theory: A Reader* (London and New York: Longman, 1988), 32-57.

tensions of sin and grace, freedom and determinism, community and autonomy, and good and evil. Because of these tensions, much can get in the way of the actual reception of the message and its comprehension. Is what is being sent being received? And, even if so, is its further transmission to other human beings, "through the ages," being sent as it was first received? Moreover are new recipients receiving it as it was sent originally? The complicated dynamics open up all kinds of difficulties and possibility for error. Nevertheless, "'words,' in the sense of human language, play an essential role in the process of revelation. The words serve to identify the revelatory events, to interpret them, to preserve their memory, and to transmit them together with their saving significance."[90]

Communication and the Transmission of Symbol[91]

Michael Polanyi (1891-1976), professor of physical chemistry and social studies, was a scientist by profession and his areas of interest and study can hardly be considered

---

[90]Dulles, "Faith and Revelation," 96.

[91]For a more in-depth exploration of communication and its influence on theology, see Paul A. Soukop, *Communication and Theology* (London: World Association for Christian Communication, 1983). See also Avery Dulles, "The Church and Communications: Vatican II and Beyond," in *The Reshaping of Catholicism: Current Challenges in the Theology of Church* (San Francisco: Harper and Row, 1988), 110-131.

theological. Yet, since his death, his insights and formulations are being considered in many disciplines, including theology. In recent years Polanyi's work has found considerable favor among, and exercised exceptional influence on, theologians. Polanyi's work on human knowledge has been extremely important for Dulles and his doctrine of symbolic mediation and revelation.[92]

As Dulles enters into the discussion of the transmission of revelation, he raises a question and states a problem.

> Assuming, then, that God must manifest Himself
> through creatures, how can He impart concrete,
> interpersonal knowledge and not simply the kind
> of abstractive, inferential knowledge that is given
> in natural theology? If God were to communicate
> by signs with clearly defined meanings, *He could*

---

[92]The influence of Polanyi upon Dulles has been suggested by this author in varying places in this text up to this point. However, Dulles himself acknowledges the influence of Polanyi in the formation of his own thought: "A glimmer of light came to me when I was able to see, with Michael Polanyi's help, the distinction between tacit and explicit knowing." See *Models of Revelation*, xviii. See also *The Craft of Theology*, 5, where Dulles writes: "Students of Michael Polanyi will find it easy to detect his influence upon this chapter."

See also Polanyi, *Personal Knowledge*, x: "Things which we can tell, we know by observing them; those that we cannot tell, we know by dwelling in them. All understanding is based on our dwelling in the particulars of that which we comprehend. Such indwelling is a participation of ours in the existence of that which we comprehend; it is Heidegger's *being-in-the-world*."

not tell us more than we could conceive and express within the categories derived from our day-to-day experience of the world. He could not give us an intimate, familiar knowledge of Himself, an awareness that transforms our lives and makes us sharers in God's own perspective on the world. Still less could such discursive, inferential knowledge take us beyond all the categories of conceptual thought and impart a share in the blessed mystery of God's own life. And yet revelation, as understood in Catholic Christianity, must accomplish all this.

[The] problem, then, is to reconcile the worldly mediation of revelation with its power to bring us into the sphere of the divine.[93]

Dulles maintains that the solution to this problem must ultimately be sought in a clear perspective on what it means for human beings "to know."

Accordingly, Dulles proposes that there are two general kinds of knowing. On the one hand, "objective knowledge," or empirical knowledge, forms the foundation for mathematical and scientific exploration and discovery. It is characterized by "observation and abstraction from the world we see about us."[94] On the other hand, there is "participatory knowledge." This

---

[93]Dulles, "The Symbolic Structure of Revelation," 60. Our emphasis.

[94]Dulles, "The Symbolic Structure of Revelation," 60.

type of knowledge finds itself outside the realm of that which can be objectively verified and is characterized by an interpretative process that is subjective in nature. The contextual arena for this type of knowledge is human relationships and human communication. To come to an awareness of another human being, that is to say, to have knowledge of another human being, involves a complex dynamic in which objective knowledge, reached through observation and abstraction, is incomplete. Dulles holds that our personal knowledge of other human beings is "achieved through interpretation of the signs—the words and gestures [the language]—by which people express themselves."[95] Moreover to understand or apprehend the true meaning of the symbols used in self-expression, "one must *pass through* the symbol to what it makes present (re-presents). This is true to an extent of all types of communication, even the indicative signs of ordinary language."[96]

---

[95] Dulles, "The Symbolic Structure of Revelation," 60. Our *inclusio*. See also Dulles, "Faith and Revelation," 109. Dulles offers a discussion of "two kinds of knowledge" from the perspective of faith and knowledge. He points out that there is "evidential knowledge," in which the individual understands the basis for an assent to the truth of the information, and "faith-knowledge," in which the individual is able to assent to the knowledge "because of the trustworthiness of a witness." He writes that a person cannot believe in what is known "evidentially." See also Dulles, *The Assurance of Things Hoped For*, 214-218.

[96] Kelly, "Knowing by Heart," 69.

The process involved in participatory knowledge is a subtle one. It is threatened by potential misinterpretation if the process takes place within an isolated and individualized context. What is necessary for true knowledge and awareness to surface and to be understood, despite the problems that are inherent in the interpretation of participatory knowledge, is a social element. It is important to recognize that knowledge has a social dimension. Dulles asserts that no one person has the ability to command all the information or evidence for solving a problem or understanding that which is symbolically communicated.[97] The relationship a person has to others and to the broader community, and the daily engagement and interaction with other people who are, by their very nature, involved in the same process of coming to know, unconsciously affects one's participatory knowledge—that is to say, the knowledge that flows from "dwelling in [the symbol], by using it, [and] by relying on it"[98] while "dwelling" in the community.

One of the important elements in the discussion of participatory knowledge, although not peculiar to it, involves the

---

[97]Dulles, *The Craft of Theology*, 6. According to Dulles, this is the fourth "flaw" inherent in the "critical era."

[98]Dulles, "The Symbolic Structure of Revelation," 60. Our *inclusio*. The concepts of "participatory knowledge" and "indwelling" are incorporated, by Dulles, into his consideration of Lindbeck's "cultural-linguistic" theory of doctrine. Dulles uses these concepts to develop his so-called "ecclesial-transformative" approach.

interpretation of the language used to express one's self or to convey particular information about one's self. Language is subject to external forces which affect its usefulness in the communicative process and the consideration of these forces is the subject of the following discussion.

Language as Socially, Culturally, and Historically Conditioned

Language is socially and culturally conditioned. The words, symbols, [and] gestures that constitute a language are the articulation, as it were, of a particular culture's attempt to define and maintain its identity and its existence. Conditioned also by history, language appropriates the insights and nuances of past generations and, more specifically, the cultural heritage of the community. Language evolves. As the environment of the symbol, language will inevitably influence the transmission of that which is to be revealed and, ultimately, that which is to become known. In any type of interpersonal communication (and revelation will be defined as such later on) the language employed must be a language that is understood and embraced by all those involved.

Language, Word and Gesture, as Symbol

For Dulles, language is ultimately symbolic. Any word spoken or written, any gesture acted out and communicated, is pregnant with meaning that goes beyond its face value. This is especially true in the act of self-communication, the self-realization of one being in and through another. Here words and gestures are rarely taken at face value, and there is usually an underlying presupposition that "more" is being communicated than "meets the eye" (or, to continue the analogy, than "enters the ear"). Part of the "more" comes from language being historically, socially, and culturally conditioned. The "more," however, is also grounded in the inner being of the person who is communicating—which affects the explicitly "intended" message and the implicitly "suggested" message—as well as the inner being of the recipient—which affects the comprehension of the concrete, explicit "words" and the understanding of the "meaning behind" the words and the gestures.

In revelation, understood as the self-communication of the divine, it is critically important to recognize the symbolic character of the mediation of the content of revelation. Dulles uses the expression "word of God" to flesh out this concept:

> The expression *word of God* applies most obviously to the spoken and written words of those who are divinely inspired to put the divine message into human language. In a broader sense, however, it is a virtual synonym for revelation. The Hebrew term for "word," *dabar* (and sometimes its Greek equivalents, *logos* and *rhema*), when applied to God, includes not only speech and writing but all the external signs by which the mind of God is communicated to

human beings. Thus the symbolic gestures of
prophets and the expressive actions of inspired
believers are forms of the word of God, insofar as
these agents are taken up in the process of God's
self-communication.[99]

Revelation and Language

Like the transmission of personal information from one
human being to another, the self-communication of the divine is
intimately tied to a language that is socially, historically and
culturally conditioned. As Dulles asserts, "the revelatory modes
of communication, then, include the order of nature, historical
events, symbolic words, interior illuminations, and propositional
statements. All of these are integral to the process of
revelation."[100] The consequences of this are far-reaching. Both
the "original" transmission of the information and the "on-going
re-transmission" of the information within the lived experience of
a particular community are influenced by factors outside the
power of either the sender or the receiver. Even the language used
to document information about the divine, within propositional
or doctrinal formula, is not exempt from these conditions. It is
necessary, therefore, to proceed with caution regarding the

---

[99]Dulles, "Faith and Revelation," 118.
[100]Dulles, "Faith and Revelation," 98. These "modes" of
communication correspond to the five models of revelation
elucidated in chapter one.

passing on of the revelation received and its documentation within the framework of a particular community.

Furthermore, Juan Luis Segundo and others suggest that, by their very nature, doctrinal statements regarding revelation can be "reworked." Segundo and other theologians maintain that, because doctrinal statements are conditioned through the elements of culture, society and history, they have the potential to be re-articulated in more current language. The aim is to break open the truth of the revelation within contemporary insights and parameters, without the possible loss or destruction of the original revelation.[101]

---

[101]For an in-depth exploration of doctrine, culturally and historically conditioned language and revelation, see Juan Luis Segundo, *The Liberation of Dogma: Faith, Revelation, and Dogmatic Teaching Authority* (Maryknoll, New York: Orbis Books, 1992).

See also George De Schrijver, "Hermeneutics and Tradition," in *Authority in the Church, Annua Nuntia Louvaniensia XXVI,* ed. Piet Fransen (Leuven: Leuven University Press, 1983), 32-47. See especially, 33: "The temporality of human existence requires that we are time and again forced to give form and articulation to an excessive mass of meaning which intrudes upon us from beyond our present standpoint of understanding . . . The grasping of meaning cannot be understood but as an ever-provisional truth-acquisition. The very idea of temporality cautions us against the presumption that a once-and-forever-established 'fixation' of truth is possible. Insights which have prove[n] true in the past ought to be regarded as replaceable by other, more refined insights, in accordance with the novel circumstances of a particular

Continued on next page

Since the self-communication of the divine to human beings can only take place within the structure of human language, this language is also the language of God. This is the very anthropological focus of revelation. "Special" revelation—that is to say, revelation given through particular historical events (salvation history), is the revelation that is manifested within the complex human context. ("General" revelation, on the other hand, finds place in the context of the natural order.) Dulles believes that "symbolic revelation thus occurs by a transaction analogously similar to that whereby human persons manifest themselves through signs, with the important difference that human persons are in principle visible, whereas God is not."[102] Furthermore, he insists that "the exceptional events of salvation

---

epoch. Human beings ought to acknowledge the dramatically provisional character of this understanding."

Dulles will begin to consider this problem, although not specifically, as we shall see in the third chapter of this work, by way of the doctrine of the *sensus fidelium* as articulated by John Henry Newman. De Schrijver, who alludes to this in the above-mentioned article (p. 42), states: "An organized religion cannot survive if it fails to keep *alive* its 'common memory' by means of rituals, religious customs, catechetics, liturgical and moral preaching, prayers, etc." Our emphasis. See Dulles, *Models of Revelation*, xii, 35; *The Craft of Theology*, 66, 18, where Dulles writes that symbols are "imbued with a plenitude or depth of meaning that surpasses the capacities of conceptual thinking and propositional speech." See also Dulles, "The Symbolic Structure of Revelation," 57; "Faith, Church, and God," 544. See finally n. 104 below.

[102]Dulles, *Models of Revelation*, 258.

history, as narrated in the Bible, serve as interpretative keys to illuminate the riddles of [human] life."[103] The anthropological dimension of revelation is clear, and any contemporary methodology for revelation must take account of this fact.

Communication as Inherent to a Methodological Approach to Revelation

According to Dulles, the theology of revelation ought to constitute the foundational theological discipline.[104] He proposes

---

[103]Dulles, "Faith and Revelation," 98. Our *inclusio.*

[104]Dulles expresses a concern that "theologians lack a common language, common goals, and common norms." He goes on to say that, "in any field of learning such radical diversity [as he perceives to be present in the current situation in the theological enterprise] would be debilitating . . . Even if agreement is not universal, there is at least a prevalent and normative methodology. Members of the [medical] profession share a common vision of what they are about. The same can hardly be said of theology today, even within a single ecclesial body, such as the Catholic Church." See *The Craft of Theology*, viii. Our *inclusiones.*

This concern is the underlying motivation for his work, *The Craft of Theology*. More specifically, it is his doctrine of symbolic communication that he believes will initiate a "common language," and offer assistance in developing "common goals and common norms." Symbolic communication, and, by extension, the perception and understanding of revelation as symbolically mediated, is the cornerstone, the foundational principle for the theological enterprise of Avery Dulles. See also Mattes, "Review of *The Craft of Theology*," 145. Mattes suggests that "the contemporary, underlying concern that Dulles is wrestling with it

Continued on next page

making it so through a theology of symbolic realism—that is to say, an approach combining Christian anthropology with an understanding of the symbol and symbolic communication. For this to happen, the formal object of theology needs to be characterized in new terms. In *The Craft of Theology* (and, here again, one detects Rahner's influence), Dulles points out that,

> in the past the formal object, or subject matter, of theology has usually been identified in terms of what God is, or has done, but not in terms of communication, considered as a sharing of conscious life. To Karl Rahner, more than others, belongs the credit for having redefined the formal object of theology in a way that brings out the communications dimension.[105]

With the formal object of theology reconceived in terms of communication, the theological stage is set to resituate revelation as foundational. The dynamics of communication are familiar and accessible to everyone. For this reason, the framework of communication offers an approach to revelation that may be, perhaps, more widely accessible than other possible approaches. Revelation is usually conceived as something powerfully transcendent, distant from the ordinary life of the believer. "All Christian believers, it could be said, tacitly know what revelation

---

the question of how to impart authentic Christian identity for future generations."

is simply by virtue of adherence to a revealed religion. But they do not yet have a formulated concept or theory of revelation."[106] The dynamics of communication, specifically, symbolic communication, offer a possibility of structural change.

> Revelation [self-communication of the divine], understood as symbolic, appears to have immediate relevancy to the believer; it seems capable of satisfying not just the mind but the whole person; it has palpable present effects and is capable of being adapted to various cultural situations. Further, the symbolic approach offers promise of contributing to a more sympathetic understanding of the faiths of other peoples.[107]

Revelation as symbolic communication has "immediate relevancy" to the believer because, once again, the human being is a symbolic being.

---

[105] Dulles, *The Craft of Theology*, 21.

[106] Dulles, *Models of Revelation*, xviii. Dulles recognizes that a "glimmer of light" came to him via the work of Michael Polanyi and the distinction between "tacit and explicit knowing," as he struggled for a methodological approach to theology (specifically revelation) that does not presuppose a doctrine of revelation and use revelation as its norm. He states that "to employ a doctrine of revelation in the very investigation of revelation would be to presuppose the answer to the very question one was asking." See *Models of Revelation*, xvii-xviii.

[107] Dulles, "The Symbolic Structure of Revelation," 57. Our *inclusio*.

Symbolic communication, as the cornerstone for a methodological approach to revelation, offers greater possibilities not only for an understanding of revelation, but also for a deeper appreciation of the self-communication of the divine and the on-going transmission of revelation in the life and lived experience of the community. It is appropriate at this point to return to Dulles' major claim—namely, that,

> God's revelation, if it is to come home [*to be communicated*] to human beings as embodied spirits, must come to expression through *tangible, social, and historically transmitted symbols*. The divine self-communication, therefore, has a social and symbolic dimension.[108]

We must now turn our attention to the symbolic and the social dimensions of this specifically divine self-communication.

---

[108]Dulles, *The Craft of Theology,* 22. Our emphasis. See also Dulles, *The Assurance of Things Hoped For,* p. 275: "It may be that if God does speak, his word will come through signs and symbols given in history and through the insights of privileged interpreters; for human life generally rises to its higher levels through socially and historically transmitted memories of striking events and through the guidance of spiritually perceptive persons."

CHAPTER THREE
REVELATION AND SYMBOL

Symbolic Communication and the Divine

The Symbolic Character of Revelation

The symbolic epistemology[109] held by Avery Dulles functions as the foundational component for his considerations regarding revelation, and by extension, all of theology. It is foundational because "the role of symbol and imagination has been neglected in most epistemologies, which have relied heavily on mathematical, empirical, and metaphysical models."[110] Dulles' epistemology incorporates not only those conceptual elements of an anthropological nature, which we addressed in the previous chapter, but also those of a theological nature. Clearly Dulles' conception of symbol is "partly

---

[110]Dulles, *The Communication of Faith and Its Content*, 7.

determined by [his] beliefs as a Christian."[111] Through his symbolic epistemology he is able to flesh out answers to the significant questions that surround revelation—for example, the self-communication of God, the means by which revelation is initially communicated, the process by which the divine self-communication comes to interact with the human being, and how the human being comes "to know" revelation and "know" truth claims of and about revelation. "A revelation that begins with symbolic communication gradually generates a whole series of reflections and interpretations that explicate its meaning."[112]

---

[111]Dulles, *Models of Revelation*, xix: "The symbolic epistemology employed in this book is consciously theological, rather than merely literary or anthropological." Dulles also writes that "just as the epistemologist writes of knowledge as one who already knows, so the theologian writes of revelation as already accepting it." See *Models of Revelation*, 265.

[112]Dulles, "Faith and Revelation," 97. It is also important to note that, for Dulles, "because [revelation] is a call to personal union with God, revelation presupposes in the human recipient a certain affinity with the infinite, the divine. Revelation is a grace, an anticipation of the blessed union to be consummated in heaven. God's word, which comes *externally* through visible and tangible signs [pregnant with a plenitude of meaning], resounds also *within*, the depths of the human consciousness." See "Faith and Revelation," 97. Our *inclusiones* and emphasis.

An Understanding of Symbolic Language and Revelation

As was asserted in Chapter Two, Dulles argues that revelation is, by its very nature, symbolic. In the development of his argument he explicates four major characteristics of symbol/symbolism and symbolic language.[113] Dulles maintains that these are, in turn, comparable to the major characteristics of revelation. Using similar language and formulations, Dulles argues that revelation "gives participatory awareness . . . is transformative . . . has an impact on [the] commitments and behavior of those who receive it . . . and gives insight into mysteries that reason can in no way fathom."[114] As in the case of the characteristics of symbol and symbolic language, we will address each one of these elements of revelation individually.

---

[113]Other theologians also suggest that "the divine self-communication 'corresponds' to *our* symbolic nature. If God wishes to communicate with *homo symbolicus*, this revelation must take a symbolic form and road. God the revealer is necessarily God the symbolizer." See Gerald O'Collins, S.J., *Retrieving Fundamental Theology: The Three Styles of Contemporary Theology* (Mahwah: Paulist Press, 1993), 99.

[114]Dulles, *Models of Revelation,* 138. Cf. Dulles, "The Symbolic Structure of Revelation," 63, 66: "Symbolic language can mediate, albeit deficiently, something of God's reality." See also O'Collins, *Retrieving Fundamental Theology,* 99-100.

Participatory Awareness

The first quality of revelation that Dulles brings to the fore is that of "participatory awareness." He states that "to accept the Christian revelation is to involve oneself in a community of faith and thus to share in the way of life marked out by Jesus."[115] He supports this proposition by highlighting a particular text from the first letter of John. "He who does not

---

[115]Dulles, *Models of Revelation,* 138. Once again it is important to note the development in Dulles' thought. In his article, "The Symbolic Structure of Revelation," 63, he speaks of three qualities of symbolic knowledge and hence three qualities of revelation, which " . . . correspond [to them] on the transcendent level . . ." Dulles suggested that the first characteristic, "participatory knowledge," is the foundational principle of revelation, from which, "as a consequence," the other three flow. In Chapter Nine of *Models of Revelation,* Dulles no longer identifies "participatory knowledge" as the foundational principle for the other three. The four elements now possess equal status.

See also Dulles, "Revelation and Discovery," 13, 23, 26, 28, especially 23-24: "The discovery cannot come to those who simply look at the facts as disinterested spectators. To be involved in the divinization process, as it radiates from Jesus, requires an existential affinity with the meaning of the events themselves."

See also O'Collins, *Retrieving Fundamental Theology,* 104: "'Participatory knowledge' serves to sum up the two inseparable but distinguishable dimensions of symbols and, specifically, religious symbols. God's self-communication through symbols entails not only meaning, knowledge and truth (= revelation) but also meaning/truth that transforms and knowledge that calls on us to participate in a new life (= redemption)."

love does not know God; for God is love"(I Jn 4:8). Dulles thus suggests that "knowledge" of God takes place through an active relationship of love—that is to say, in and through the religious quest for God and in faith and the worship of God. This religious quest takes place only in, and through, an active participation in a community of faith. Only by "living in," "attending from," "dwelling in," and "participating in" the life of a community of faith that accepts the revelation of Christ can one becomes aware of the manifestation of the divine.[116] The life of Jesus, as symbolic revelation, gives the participant "knowledge" about Jesus, about God through Jesus, about his interaction with his followers and his call to discipleship, and by extension, about the early Christian community and their active participation in this same revelation. The life of Jesus becomes a touchstone for the lived experience of the community of Jesus and a stepping stone to knowledge and understanding that lies beyond so-called objective human knowing.[117] The requirement, however, is *participation,* not just theoretical assent.

---

[116]See Dulles, *The Craft of Theology,* 18, 19, 20, 24, 26, 28, 34-38, 65; *The Reshaping of Catholicism,* 85, 86, 88; "Faith and Revelation," 117, 122; *The Communication of Faith and Its Content,* 14-17.

[117]See Dulles, "Revelation and Discovery," 21-24, especially 23: "The mere fact of Christ, taken as an objective certifiable occurrence, is not yet revelation, but when met by a believing interpretation [through participation in a community of faith] which captures its true significance, it becomes revelation in a special and altogether unique sense. God's self-revelation in Jesus

Continued on next page

Transformative Effects

With a formulation similar to the one he uses in his discussion of symbolic language, Dulles states that the second inherent quality of revelation is its "transformative nature." Revelation "introduces us into a new spiritual world, shifts our horizons, our perspective, our point of view."[118] Dulles suggests that biblical language speaks most clearly and is most representative of the transforming effects of revelation. Biblical imagery, with its references to God's covenant with his people, the call to repentance, the healing powers of Jesus, conversion and μετανοια, etc., unquestionably addresses the new spiritual world and the shifts in horizons and perspectives.

Moreover, human beings who assent to this revelation and "live with" it find themselves with new identities, new self-

---

therefore comes to fulfillment only in the human discovery whereby it is received." See also Dulles, *A Church to Believe In*, 44.

See also Kelly, "Knowing by Heart," 67-68, 69-72, especially 72: "This is precisely the power of symbol, that they are able to present and communicate knowledge which exceeds the receivers conscious awareness."

[118]Dulles, *Models of Revelation*, 138. Cf. Dulles, "The Symbolic Structure of Revelation," 63. See also Polanyi, *Personal Knowledge*, xi: "Indwelling is being-in-the-world [Heideggerian terminology]. Every act of tacit knowing shifts our existence, re-directing, contracting our participation in the world."

understandings and new awarenesses;[119] "For all who are led by the Spirit of God are children of God (Rm 8:15)." Through this imagery, both the community and the individual come to recognize themselves in a personal relationship with God. All are transformed by the reality of the revelation as it plays itself out in their lives.

Impact on Commitments and Conduct

The third attribute of revelation articulated by Dulles is its "impact" on the life of the recipient, the one who assents to the revelation. This impact is a consequence of its transformative nature. "If revelation came simply as abstract propositional truth or historical information, the act of faith by which it was accepted could be a merely theoretical assent. But if revelation is symbolic truth, the act by which it is accepted must express itself in conduct."[120] That is, there must be a progression from a

---

[119]See Dulles, *A Church to Believe In*, 44-46, especially 44: "Christians are convinced that through a faith-relationship to Christ they are led into a richer, more meaningful existence." See also Dulles, "Revelation and Discovery," 12, 13-18, 19, 27; *The Craft of Theology,* 22. See also O'Collins, *Retrieving Fundamental Theology*, 104.

[120]Dulles, *Models of Revelation,* 138. "'The obedience of faith' (Rom. 16:26; Cf. 1:5; 2 Cor. 10:5-6) must be given to God who reveals, an obedience by which man entrusts his whole self freely to God . . ." See *DV 5*. See also Dulles, "Faith and

Continued on next page

new self-awareness or self-identity, as an individual or as a community of faith, to the expression or living out of this new identity. This new identity is integrally connected with responsibilities and commitments that flow from the revelation that is Christ.

> Christianity, then, should not be seen simply as discovery or revelation. Under the conditions of this life it is constituted more prominently by faith. The first Christians were well advised when they spoke of their movement as "the Way" ([η‘ όδος] - Acts 9:2; 18:26; 19:9, 23; 24:22). They were convinced that under the guidance of Jesus they were on the path to truth and life (Cf. Jn 14:6).[121]

Revelation," 104-106, 114-116; *The Communication of Faith and Its Content*, 14-17.

See also Kelly, "Knowing by Heart," 82: "The symbols of faith, therefore, not only reveal the mystery of God, but in so doing reveal believers to themselves, as persons oriented to the mystery. This brings with it the invitation—and obligation—for them to commit themselves in freedom to the mystery and to that which reveals it: to affirm it, to rely on it, to recreate its presence continually so that its influence can permeate their lives."

[121]Dulles, "Revelation and Discovery," 25. See Dulles, *A Church to Believe In*, 44-45: "By placing themselves [members of a community of faith] under the lordship of Christ they acquire standards and goals, they can labor with new intensity, find deeper communion with others who share the same faith, and be constantly challenged to become their own best selves." See also Dulles, *The Craft of Theology*, 22.

Consequently, revelation as symbolic truth is, intimately connected with discipleship. Moreover, when the individual, or community, is transformed by *revelation* being "played out" in their lives, this *new identity,* when actualized in their commitments and behaviors—that is to say, in their moral lives—makes further transformation and conversion possible.

Insight into Mysteries

Finally, according to Dulles, revelation "gives *insight* into mysteries that reason can in no way fathom . . . Revelation is itself a mystery inasmuch as it is the self-communication of the God 'who dwells in unapproachable light' (I Tim 6:16)."[122] This characteristic is quite similar to the fourth element of symbolic language—offering new realms of awareness—in that there is a recognition of the bi-polar dimension of revelation, the simultaneous revelation and concealment of that, or, in this case, who, is being revealed. The symbol, as we have seen, draws one

---

[122]Dulles, *Models of Revelation,* 138. Our emphasis. See Dulles, "Revelation and Discovery," 6, 11, 12; see especially 25: "Because the fullness of vision remains a distant hope, the revelation given in this life falls short of clarity. It is not the vision, but stands in place of that vision. In other words, it is pro-visional." See also Dulles, "Faith, Reason, and the Logic of Discovery," *The Survival of Dogma* (New York: Crossroad, 1987), 44-59.

into a multifaceted milieu of possible meaning. This involves a recognition that while some particular facet of meaning may come to the surface for one person, it may not necessarily come to the surface for another. Furthermore, while one particular facet of meaning comes to the surface, other possibilities may continue to remain hidden. The meanings which appear are dependent on the individual and on the intensity of the indwelling.

That which is revealed as revelation is, at the same time, concealed because it is of God. Dulles returns, once again, to the theology of symbol of Paul Tillich, noting that Tillich, along with many theologians involved in "symbolic theology," characterizes revelation primarily by its mysterious nature. Tillich argues that, "in being revealed, [the transcendent] does not cease to remain concealed, since its secrecy pertains to its very essence; and when it is revealed it is so precisely as that which is hidden."[123] Dulles goes on to highlight that Vatican I, in the document *Dei Filius*, asserted the same concept:

---

[123]Paul Tillich, *"Die Idee der Offenbarung,"* in *Zeitschrift für Theologie und Kirche: Der neuen Folge 8* (Tübingen: Mohr, 1927), 403-413 at 406: *"Es hört dadurch, daß es sich offenbart, nicht auf, verborgen zu sein; denn seine Verborgenheit gehört zu seinem Wesen; und wenn es offenbar wird, so wird auch dieses offenbar, daß es das Verborgene ist."* Quoted in English by Dulles, *Models of Revelation,* 138-139. See also Dulles, "The Symbolic Nature of Revelation," 63-64. Dulles' *inclusio.* See also Dulles, *The Craft of Theology,* 23, 26-27, 37-38.

> Divine mysteries of their very nature so excel the
> created intellect that even when they have been
> given in revelation and accepted in faith, that very
> faith still keeps them veiled in a sort of obscurity,
> as long as 'we are exiled from the Lord' in this
> mortal life, 'for we walk by faith and not by
> sight' (2 Cor. 5:6-7).[124]

Nevertheless, Dulles is quick to declare that "the mysterious
character of revelation . . . does not deprive it of intelligibility,
for as Vatican Council I asserted in the paragraph just quoted,
'reason, enlightened by faith, . . . achieves with God's help a
certain understanding, and indeed a very fruitful one,' of the
divine mysteries."[125] The intelligibility of revelation, this certain
understanding of the divine self-communication, becomes both
the structure and the power, so to speak, of the symbolic
language to engage the human being in the symbol itself. In turn,
the symbol becomes the very door through which the
actualization of the inherent transforming effects of revelation, in
its impact on the behavior and commitment of the human being,
can take place.

Dulles, it seems, has argued successfully for the
realization that revelation and symbolic language possess a key
structural relationship. This relationship allows the union

---

[124]*Dei Filius*, Chapter 4, (DS 3016).
[125]Dulles, *Models of Revelation*, 139. See also Dulles, "The
Symbolic Structure of Revelation," 63-64.

between God and humanity to become more intimate—intimate in that humanity, through the symbolic self-disclosure of the divine, is capable of coming to a deeper awareness of God's presence and God's language. Dulles writes:

> Since symbol, as we have seen, invites participation, a revelation imparted through symbol does not leave the recipient passive, but tends to elicit a high degree of spiritual activity. The plasticity of symbol gives it a power to speak to people of different sociocultural situations and to assure that revelance [*sic*] is not lost.[126]

This "plasticity" of symbolic language alerts us to the broader reality in and through which revelation occurs. In this broader context of reality, the social dimensions of revelation are made clear—the central social element focusing on the relational dynamics between God and humanity as well as within the community itself. Having come to a detailed identification of the parallel structure between symbol and symbolic language and revelation, we must move into a more specific exploration of God's self-disclosure within the context of symbolic language.

---

[126]Dulles, *Models of Revelation,* 153. The word should read "relevance."

God's Self-Disclosure and Symbolic Realism

Throughout this inquiry into God's self disclosure to human beings, we have set forth the proposition that, in the act of revelation, God communicates knowledge (and/or awareness) of what normally lies beyond human perception. This knowledge/awareness can involve "information" about both the divine Other and the relationship between the divine and human beings with insight into the reality that forms the context of that experience. Furthermore, this information also involves the human being itself. Revelation, as an act of divine self-disclosure thus becomes an act of human self-discovery. Symbol and symbolic language, therefore, function as the medium for communication and discovery.

> The concreteness of the symbol enables us to participate in the experience of another (here, a divine Other) in ways that are beyond the scope of ordinary discursive speech, which tends toward separation and abstraction. Symbols do not merely instruct us, but invite us to share a feeling, a perception of reality through the heart.[127]

---

[127]Kelly, "Knowing by Heart," 68. In his reflections on Dulles' symbolic theology, Kelly also asks if this kind of "knowledge" really requires a revelation. He concludes that "revelation occurs precisely to give assurance to our wavering
Continued on next page

This perception of reality, especially the participation in the experience of another, is what helps create a recognition of the very symbolic nature of revelation.

Justin Kelly considers the problem regarding the requirements for the recognition of the symbolic character of revelation. He highlights the "awareness of both the unity and the difference between the reality symbolized and the forms which mediate it."[128] The awareness of "the unity and the difference" is central to the acknowledgement that symbol by itself is not revelation. Simply put, revelation is inherently symbolic, but symbol and symbolism are not inherently revelatory.

---

heart-testimony, to put the weight of God's truth behind it. Revelation occurs to show us what God loves."

This "participation in the experience of another" is reminiscent of both Polanyi and Rahner. See Dulles, "Revelation and Discovery," 1-29; "Faith, Reason, and the Logic of Discovery," 44-59. See Rahner, *"Zur Theologie des Symbols,"* 275-311, especially, 296. ["The Theology of the Symbol," 235-245, especially 239]: "Every God-given reality, where it has not been degraded to a purely human tool and to merely utilitarian purposes, states much more than itself: each in its own way is an echo and indication of all reality." Furthermore, at 290 [234]: "symbolic reality *is the self-realization of a being in the other . . .*" See also Dulles, *The Communication of Revelation and Its Content,* 8-9.

[128]Kelly, "Knowing by Heart," 69.

In the light of this, a number of Dulles' other claims regarding the symbolic character of revelation become clear. Dulles maintains that,

> revelation never occurs in a purely internal experience or as an unmediated encounter with God. It is always mediated through an experience in the world. More specifically, it is mediated through symbol [the "real"]—that is to say, through an externally perceived sign that works mysteriously on the human consciousness so as to suggest more than it can clearly describe or define. Revelatory symbols are those which express and mediate God's self-communication.[129]

---

[129]Dulles, "The Symbolic Structure of Revelation," 55-56. Our *inclusio.* Cf. Dulles, *Models of Revelation,* 131. Dulles also speaks of "revelatory symbols" in a significant number of places throughout the text. See, for example, 11, 131, 139-140, 144, 258, 260-267, 269.

In *Models of Revelation*, 35, Dulles writes, that with a "typological approach" to revelation, typologists understand revelation to be, in some degree, ineffable and that "every effort to say what revelation is must rely on inadequate metaphors and therefore falls short of the reality. Revelation is known when it occurs, but this knowledge, given in the depth of the human spirit, should never be confused with statements about revelation."

Moreover, the symbolic language used to articulate the human experience of revelation could be described as "first order language" while the theological statements *about* revelation, or the reflection upon the primary experience could be described as "second order language." See Dulles, *The Craft of Theology*, 19. See

Continued on next page

In other words, revelatory symbols bespeak a symbolic reality. Consequently, as Kelly expresses it, the essence of revelation consists in an understanding of how one comes to know something as,

> the result of a divine initiative—a meaning not made but disclosed. However much human inquiry, observation, and effort have paved the way for it, it occurs freely and unexpectedly. It is beyond human control, and the halo of wonder surrounding it is already a glimpse of God.[130]

It becomes evident that revelation is a process. This process involves the divine initiative but only within the human framework of men and women who are able to question, to seek, and to explore. Consequently, as Kelly rightly maintains, this process of revelation,

> involves a kind of self-realization . . . on the part of the one who receives the revelation, a symbolic

---

also Michael L. Cook, S.J., "Revelation As Metaphoric Process," *Theological Studies 47* (1986), 388-411, especially 390-391.

[130]Kelly, "Knowing by Heart," 73. Kelly also cites Dulles' article "Revelation and Discovery," 1-29. Kelly notes that, in "Revelation and Discovery," Dulles shows "that the apparent opposition of 'acquired' and 'revealed' knowledge is not as absolute as this facile dichotomy suggests." See Kelly's footnote 14, located at 212.

self-recognition. [And yet, at the same time] there exists in every human being a hunger for God that is already a dark foreknowledge of the one sought.[131]

It is, as it were, a sort of *a priori* dynamic. Revelation involves the divine initiative. It leads to human self-awareness and self-understanding. Yet what is implicit in the very nature of the human being is a longing for the divine, a longing that opens up the possibility for the divine initiative, God's self-communication, by providing an environment through which it can be actualized. This environment, according to Dulles, is the place where the world of symbol and symbolic language come alive.

Symbolic Realism— Faith as an Openness to Symbol

Revelation, understood as the articulation of the divine self, manifests itself in two significant realms of reality: that of symbol and that of human consciousness. "God's word, which comes *externally* through visible and tangible signs, resounds also

---

[131]Kelly, "Knowing by Heart," 73. The "dark foreknowledge of the one sought," of which Kelly speaks, suggests the Rahnerian concept of *Vorgriff,* the unthematic awareness. We return to this notion in the following sections.

within, in the depths of the human consciousness."[132] Nevertheless Dulles does not contend that revelation is to be identified as or equated with symbol. Accordingly, he describes revelation as the "self-manifestation of God through a form of communication that could be termed, at least in a broad sense, symbolic."[133] This helps clarify the notion of "symbolic realism" espoused by Dulles—that is to say, the specific demands presented by a Christian interpretation of symbol and symbolism. The notion of symbolic realism, Dulles maintains, characteristically identifies symbol by virtue of the influence placed upon it by the Christian tradition. The paradigm of symbolic realism suggests that "the true content of Christianity is the joint meaning of the Christian symbols—a meaning that

---

[132]Dulles, "Faith and Revelation," 97. Our emphasis. See also Dulles, *The Craft of Theology,* 23: "Any revelatory sign or symbol may be called, in a generic sense, the word of God. As word it has three dimensions, corresponding to the three 'persons' recognized in grammar. In its first-person dimension the word is an expressive symbol, manifesting the previously hidden thoughts and attitudes of the speaker. In its second-person dimension the word is address: it summons others to hear and be attentive. In its third-person dimension the word has a content: something is communicated . . . Without all these three dimensions a theology of revelation would be incomplete. God by his symbolic action manifests himself as revealer; he summons human beings to be attentive and responsive; and he gives them *ideas and insights that they would otherwise lack.*" Our emphasis.

[133]Dulles, *Models of Revelation*, 266. See also Dulles, *The Craft of Theology*, 20-22, especially 20.

can never be adequately formulated in language, but is tacitly perceived through reliance on the symbols themselves."[134] Dulles elucidates five points inherent to symbolic realism.[135]

Dulles' first element of symbolic realism points to the idea that "revelatory symbols are not pure creations of the human imagination."[136] The fundamental symbols of Christian revelation are historical personages or events that become the instruments by which God *calls into existence the community of faith.*[137] Dulles explains, however, that on the basis of these self-manifestations, God may also inspire believers to construct images that are helpful for understanding and communicating what has been given in revelation. It is necessary to appreciate the fact that revelatory symbols can function on two levels. They function both on the primary level, the initial communication of the divine, and on the secondary level, the level of explanation and on-going transmission of the initial disclosure. Human beings may find it necessary to use other

---

[134]Dulles, *The Communication of Faith and Its Content*, 11.
[135]Dulles, *Models of Revelation*, 264, 266-267.
[136]Dulles, *Models of Revelation*, 266. See also Dulles, *The Communication of Faith and Its Content*, 15, 12, 9. Dulles writes, that "Jesus Christ, in the Christian understanding, is a symbol: not indeed a fictitious or merely literal symbol produced by the free operation of human fantasy, but a real symbol (or symbolic reality) constituted by God's action in history." See also Dulles, "The Symbolic Structure of Revelation," 57.
[137]Dulles, *Models of Revelation*, 266. See also Dulles, *The Craft of Theology*, 33-35, 65.

symbols and symbolic language to *express* the revelation of God, but these are, as Dulles suggests, "secondary"—that is to say, not the symbolic manifestation of the divine, only its interpretation.

The second element of symbolic realism involves the recognition that "Christian revelation is not simply the product of human interpretation of the natural symbols contained in cosmic nature. Through specific actions at definite points in time and place, the universal symbolism of nature is taken up into the biblical and Christian tradition and thereby given added depth and significance."[138] There exists a critical interplay between the created world of nature and the cosmos, and the course of human and biblical history. More specifically, only through this interplay between the created world-order and the tradition[139], do the symbols found in nature take on revelatory proportions. The interaction involves an "appropriation" of the natural symbol, not solely an "interpretation" of it.

---

[138]Dulles, *Models of Revelation,* 266. See Dulles, *The Craft of Theology,* 19, 28-29, 33-35; "Faith, Church, and God," 545-546; "The Symbolic Structure of Revelation," 64; *The Communication of Faith and Its Content,* 6-7, 8.

[139]This fundamental idea of tradition will be explored in greater detail in the following chapter. At this point it is sufficient to note that, in this context, Dulles understands tradition to be the lived history of the community of faith. See Dulles, *The Craft of Theology,* 87-104; "Faith and Revelation," 120-123.

Thirdly, it is to be understood that "symbols do not necessarily point to things strictly other than themselves."[140] In other words, Dulles suggests that the *possibility* exists that the symbol and the symbolized are uniquely one. He maintains however, that ". . . there must be at least a formal distinction between the symbol and what it points to." To substantiate this point, Dulles refers to *Lumen Gentium*'s claim that just as the two natures of Christ, his human nature and his nature as divine λογος, form a "single interlocked reality,"[141] so also, the Church's structural and sacramental dimensions form a "single interlocked reality." Dulles calls these kinds of symbols "'realizing symbols'— symbols that contain and mediate the reality they signify."[142]

---

[140]Dulles, *Models of Revelation,* 266. See also Dulles, *The Craft of Theology*, 26-27.

[141]Dulles, *Models of Revelation*, 266-267. LG, no. 8, " *Una realitas complexa.*" It would appear that this characteristic of symbolic realism is influenced in part by Rahner's understanding of the "unity and multiplicity of being" in symbol. The reader is referred back to footnote 62 found in Chapter Two of this work. See also Dulles, *The Communication of Faith and Its Content,* 8.

[142]Dulles, *Models of Revelation*, 267. Dulles speaks of "realizing" or "real" symbols in many places throughout this text. See, for example, 157, 159, 218, 267, 295. The distinction to be made here, between symbols and "realizing symbols," is that Dulles suggests that the symbols do not "necessarily" point to things other than themselves." See n. 140. There is, for Dulles, the possibility that "symbols" like "Christ" and the "Church" are "actualizations" of the reality beyond the symbol—that is to say, the reality is "realized" in the symbol.

Continued on next page

As the fourth dimension of symbolic realism, Dulles also contends that "revelatory symbols do not simply arouse emotions, strivings, fantasies, and ideals. They point to, and provide insight into, *realities* inaccessible to direct human experience. Although they are not scale models, pictures, or descriptions of what they signify, such symbols denote and disclose what is *ontologically real*."[143]

The fifth element of symbolic realism concerns the inherent truth-categories involved in the symbols that are the media of the manifestation of the divine self. Dulles holds that,

> revelatory symbols . . . have a twofold truth. They have "symbolic truth" insofar as they express, communicate, or produce a transformed consciousness. But the truth of the symbol is not merely its symbolic truth. In reflection, symbols [also] give rise to true affirmations about what is

---

See also Rahner, *"Zur Theologie des Symbols,"* 297-299. ["The Theology of the Symbol," 240-241.] Rahner speaks of the Church and *Logos* as revelatory symbols, "revelatory because the symbol renders present what is revealed."

[143]Dulles, *Models of Revelation*, 267. Our emphasis. See also Dulles, *The Craft of Theology,* 22, 31-32, 37-39; *The Communication of Faith and Its Content,* 9: "Faith rises to its greatest achievements when the mind takes advantage of the signs and symbols handed down in the community of faith. It receives these from the Church which faithfully transmits them. Then, through an assent of mind and heart the believer deepens his or her grasp on the *truth revealed to us by God in these signs and symbols* and thus grows in faith." Our emphasis.

antecedently real. Revelatory symbols, being dense and concrete, can generate an inexhaustible brood of affirmations. Yet the symbols are not indefinitely malleable. Only some statements can claim to be grounded in the symbols; certain others are excluded by the symbols, rightly understood.[144]

Symbols are, in other words, powerful conveyors of the truth of the divine self-manifestation to humanity. It may be suggested, however, that because of the multivalent character of symbol, and the attendant possibility of a multiplicity of interpretations, the symbol cannot be the articulation of *any* possible truth claims. Dulles would clearly reject this suggestion. It is *because* of their multifarious nature that symbols are capable of expressing that which is true concerning revelation. He cautions, however, that all affirmations or statements that claim to possess truth are conditioned by the very symbol itself and the history

---

[144]Dulles, *Models of Revelation,* 267. Our emphasis. Dulles maintains, throughout his considerations of symbol, that symbols are not "indefinitely malleable." See also Dulles, *Models of Revelation,* 153, 154. Dulles also notes that the distinction for the fifth characteristic of symbol, its "twofold truth," namely, its "symbolic truth" and "the truth of the symbol," is made by Wilbur M. Urban in *Language and Reality* (London: Allen & Unwin, 1939), 444.

See Dulles, "The Symbolic Structure of Revelation," 63; "Faith, Church, and God," 545-546; *The Communication of Faith and Its Content,* 9.

of the community of faith. These statements must be concomitant with the community's history of experience of the divine. The interpretation of the symbol is not without limits— limits that find articulation within the very life of faith through which the symbol finds expression.

Dulles acknowledges the variety of revelatory symbols— that is to say, of Christian symbolism—and offers some examples to support his notion of symbolic realism. In fact, Dulles develops a three-fold typology of symbolism; symbols identified as cosmic, historic or sacramental. *Light* is one of the most significant and easily recognized revelatory symbols identified within the Christian tradition. An example of the first type of symbolism, namely, "cosmic or nature symbolism"[145] is light. Light has always been closely connected with understanding, insight, and knowledge in both the secular world and in the religious realm (God represented as "light from the heavens;" Jesus as the "light of the world," John 8:12; etc.).

Dulles' second type of Christian symbolism is the symbolism exemplified by the *cross*. Dulles situates this in the

---

[145]Dulles, *Models of Revelation,* 139. Dulles uses two words—"type" and "kind"—in setting up this three-fold typology for symbolism found in symbolic realism. In this discussion he offers one example of each such "type" of symbolism.

See also Dulles, "Faith and Revelation," 98; "Revelation and Discovery," 11. Here, the quote from Augustine (see footnote 51 of Chapter One of this work) surfaces in the context of the
Continued on next page

category of "historical symbolism."[146] As the symbol, for all intents and purposes, most central to the Christian faith, the cross expresses keenly the multifarious nature of symbol. Dulles points out that it has the power to suggest meanings that range from the natural plane (an intersection on a road, and by extension, decisions to be made), through the "objective" plane (the cross as a wooden object to be "carried"). The cross has the power to continue on into the scriptural realm of the Gospels (where it is seen as crucifixion or punishment, and, from the point of view of Jesus, as love for sinners and God's commitment to humanity, reconciliation), and up through the history of the Christian tradition until the present day (where the cross is seen as a "sign" of identification and commitment to faith in Christ Jesus).[147]

Dulles proposes yet a third type of symbolism— *sacramental worship and ritual*.[148] Each of the sacraments,

---

"interrogation of the order of nature," in the search for, and discovery of, God.

[146]Dulles, *Models of Revelation,* 139. See also Dulles, "Faith and Revelation," 98. See Kelly, "Knowing by Heart," 72-73, 78-79.

[147]Dulles, *Models of Revelation*, 139-140.

[148]Dulles, *Models of Revelation*, 140. See Dulles, "Faith, Church, and God," 545-546: Dulles writes that, for Polanyi, and Dulles believes Polanyi to be correct, religious worship is a "heuristic performance," a process that involves "disposing the worshiper to be carried away in contemplation . . . The mind, dwelling in the clues afforded by the symbolic texts and gestures (including those which Christians call sacraments) enters into an

Continued on next page

within the Catholic Christian perspective, including the rituals which surround them, possesses a multiplicity of meaning that is profoundly extensive. This extensiveness of meaning is reflected in the acknowledgement that the revelation expressed, and the unity with the divine experienced, far exceeds any one, single dimension, categorization, or articulation. Yet this is true of all revelatory symbols. In the case of sacramental worship and ritual, however, the symbols become "living symbols." They embrace both the expression and articulation of the truth, *and* the on-going transmission of the truth, of the divine self-manifestation.

Kelly offers some further insight into Dulles' understanding of symbol. Utilizing Dulles' schema of symbolic realism, he notes that:

---

affective relationship with God, who is foreknown, so to speak, in the passionate longing to contemplate Him."

See also Dulles, *The Communication of Faith and Its Content,* 15-16. See Kelly, "Knowing by Heart," 79-81. See Dulles, *The Craft of Theology* [Expanded Edition, 1995], 197. Dulles asserts that liturgy is recognized as a "prime theological source." He states that "if theology relies on symbolic communication as heavily as I [Dulles] have maintained in my second chapter [of this text], situations of worship in which the word of God is reverently heard, and in which the faithful participate in sacramental worship, deserve fuller treatment that I have given them thus far." Consequently, the additional chapter, "Theology and Worship," looks more closely at this theme.

These statements [words like "I AM," "the Christ," and phrases like "I believe in one God," or "Jesus Christ is Lord"] reveal God, therefore, in their very density and mystery-laden obscurity; they are verbal symbols for what necessarily surpasses human comprehension and conceptual articulation. To say this is not to say that revelation has no intelligible content . . . But their literal meaning is not their whole or even their primary meaning. For them to be truly a revelation *of God*, they must "say" more than human language as such can ever convey.[149]

Dulles, in drawing his own conclusions on symbolic realism, writes:

All three of the symbols here used as examples may be said to possess an indefinite range of potential significations, many of them deeply ingrained in the archetypal forms of human consciousness. It would be futile to search in any of these symbols for some one lesson or articulate meaning. Because of their capacity to integrate a multitude of lofty speculations and half-felt sentiments, symbols have an integrative and

---

[149]Kelly, "Knowing by Heart," 66-67. Cf. Dulles, *Models of Revelation*, 144, 153.

reconciling power far greater than any explicit statement.[150]

However "futile" it may be to search for one meaning, the evidence is clear regarding meaning in and of itself. These symbols not only represent, or point to, something beyond themselves, but, in very real and concrete ways, can, and do, give expression to the divine-self.

Social and Symbolic Dimensions of the Divine Self-Communication

By now it has become critically clear that ". . . revelation is not merely knowledge *about* God; it is the very being of God, symbolically bestowed."[151] This is the first dynamic aspect of revelation understood as a symbolic process. Utilizing Dulles' language, Kelly emphasizes that "revelation is a symbolic process in that the concrete signs through which God is manifested [are] necessarily other than God."[152]

---

[150]Dulles, *Models of Revelation,* 141. See also Dulles, *The Craft of Theology*, 18, 19, 21.

[151]Kelly, "Knowing by Heart," 70.

[152]Kelly, "Knowing by Heart," 70. See also Rahner, *"Zur Theologie des Symbols,"* 293-294, 296, 297-298, 299-300. ["The Theology of the Symbol," 237, 239, 240, 241.]

Revelation, understood as such, involves a second dynamic aspect—namely, the recognition of the development of the life of faith of the individual and the community.

> [Revelation] is not only the self-expression of God but the self-realization of faith. Revelation designates the process by which faith, as a trustful foreknowledge of God, comes to explicit self-recognition and objectification. In that process . . . faith transcends itself through its encounter with external signs, arriving at a new knowledge both of God and of itself. It comes to know experientially what it formally believed only notionally, or at most half-knew.[153]

Dulles summarizes the critical dimensions of symbol and revelation as follows:

> . . . Symbol can have an objective density, imposing demands on the subject to pursue its meaning as *a clue to the nature of reality* [the social dimension]. *Religious symbols claim to be based on the permanent structures of being* [the

---

[153]Kelly, "Knowing by Heart," 70-71. For an exploration of the notion of the "symbolic structure of faith" and its three facets, namely, seeking-symbol-significance, and its inherent psychological process, see "Knowing by Heart, 74-76. Kelly maintains that this "symbolic structure of faith" is essential for "receiving" revelation. See also Dulles, *The Assurance of Things Hoped For*, 217.

symbolic dimension]. The historical symbolism of biblical history, moreover, manifests the singular deeds of love whereby God has effectively transformed the possibilities of existence in the world. These symbols are not subject to arbitrary change and reinterpretation. The *constellation of symbols transmitted* [the symbolic dimension] within the Christian Tradition *imposes a discipline* [the social dimension] on new [and existing] members of the Church as they are initiated [and grow as a "pilgrim people"] into *the world of meaning intended by the symbols* [the symbolic dimension].[154]

---

[154]Dulles, *Models of Revelation,* 153. Our emphasis and *inclusiones.* Dulles goes on to say that, "dogma . . . can give stability and added power to the symbolism of primary religious discourse. The primacy of symbol does not justify any symbolic reductionism that would disallow the more reflective discourse of church doctrine and theology." See also Dulles, "Faith and Revelation," 98: "Christian doctrines set limits to the kinds of significance that can be found in the Christian symbols. The doctrines, however, are not independent revelation; they live off the power of the symbols."

Furthermore, the two-fold dynamic of the process of revelation is manifest on many levels. In the first instance, for every act of self-communication by the divine there is, at the same time, a corresponding act of self-awareness on the part of the human being. In the second instance, revelation is not only a symbolic disclosure of information *about* God but real disclosure of the divine self. Moreover, revelation is understood to be revelation of God and, as such, affects the development of faith. Finally, revelation is characterized by its social and symbolic dimensions.

It is quite evident that God's revelation must come to be realized through "tangible, social, and historically transmitted symbols" if human beings are to be in a position to understand the divine self-communication. Moreover, the social dynamic of revelation is recognized, most clearly, when revelation is received, when it "reaches its term"—that is to say, when the individual, in an interior act of assent, comes to believe, and manifests the assent with external expressions of faith. Revelation acquires public, historical, and "on-going" symbolic manifestations when it engages the community of faith which is responsible for its further transmission. It will be to our benefit if we briefly recapitulate the social and symbolic dimensions of revelation.

The Social Dimensions of Revelation

Dulles' reflections on the social dimensions of revelation depart from the supposition that human beings are social beings and that their symbolic language, used in self-expression, is historically and culturally, that is to say, socially, conditioned. Nevertheless, "the symbols of Christian revelation . . . are not indefinitely pliable. Yet they allow a desirable margin of interpretation and application, and are modified and enriched by successive recontextualizations."[155]   It   is   the

---

[155]Dulles, *Models of Revelation,* 153. Dulles points out (pp. 153-154) that, "the major biblical symbols are transmitted in the context of mutable secondary symbols, such as those employed in
Continued on next page

"recontextualization" of the symbol that can be identified as its "social conditioning," which in turn, calls forth a response of faith from the members of the community. The symbols and, if necessary, their re-interpretation, must be perceived as credible and enduring. They are to be situated only within the context of a believing, faith-filled community whose members are consciously aware of God's continued "social" activity in their midst.

These last comments highlight yet another element of the social dimension of revelation. This dimension concerns the symbol's *relationship* to, and within, a community of faith. The social dimension of revelation is also reflected in the fact that it is "transformative and has an impact on behavior and

---

Christian art and liturgy. These secondary symbols, when they cease to make the intended impact, can be replaced by others, freshly generated by the religious imagination under the impact of the central symbols of [the Christian] faith." Our *inclusio*.

Dulles points out that, with this being said, an objection is raised that bespeaks a concern over the consequent loss of our Christian "identity." Is it not possible that Christianity becomes an ever-changing "movement" rather than a constant faith enduring through time? Dulles points out that the "hypothesis" is not self-evidently true. In addressing the "hypothesis" and concern, Dulles posits that, at the present, the possibility that religion is an inherent, "permanent feature of the human condition" cannot be ruled out. It is, therefore, possible that there is a "single goal" and, hence, "a single symbol." This becomes the *entrée*, for Dulles, into an exploration into "Christ the Summit of Revelation." We will address this material in the final section of this chapter. See also Dulles, "Faith and Revelation," 96, 98.

commitment." Dulles insists that "public revelation, in the sense of a divine manifestation directed to a community of faith, is scarcely conceivable apart from social symbols which permit the sharing of the spiritual experience that defines such a community."[156]

The Symbolic Dimensions of Revelation

The prophets and the psalmists in Old Testament literature, the scriptural authors of the New Testament—most specifically the author of the vividly symbolic Book of Revelation—and other religious poets, writers and artists have been, and continue to be, familiar with the intimate connection between symbol and revelation. Because revelatory symbols render present what they reveal, the divine, they arouse and illuminate the intrinsic desire for knowledge of the divine. In turn, the same revelatory symbols carry the recipient, who places himself or herself at their disposal to a higher plane of awareness and experience of the divine self. This awareness, and, more importantly, the experience as such, deepens the desire for more knowledge. Thus the cycle continues. And, as stated earlier, this awareness is not only information *about* God but, at the same time, is also a very intimate *glimpse* into the essence of

---

[156]Dulles, "The Symbolic Structure of Revelation," 57. See also Dulles, "Faith and Revelation," 117-123; *The Communication of Faith and Its Content*, 17, 9, 10-11, 14.

God. The connection between knowledge of God and the essence of God rests squarely on a faith-filled recognition of divine symbolic-self-communication. To a member of a community of faith that espouses a position of trustful openness to the revelatory symbols of its tradition, "the God who *is* becomes a God who *acts*, acting precisely through those to whom the revelation takes place."[157]

Conversion as the Transformative Element of Revelation

One of the four major elements that characterize symbol and symbolic language is the transformative effect they have on the human being. Dulles contends that "symbols are products of the transformed consciousness, projections or constructions that express the immediate action of God on the human spirit. Besides manifesting religious experience, symbols serve to sensitize people to the presence of the divine in their own lives."[158] Revelation involves a process of illumination, as it

---

[157]Kelly, "Knowing by Heart," 71.

[158]Dulles, *The Craft of Theology*, 18. It is important to point out that these particular thoughts regarding symbol and their transformative effects are seen here within the framework of George Lindbeck's second categorization—namely, the experiential-expressive. See Lindbeck, *The Nature of Doctrine*, 16, 31-32. The fact remains that, although symbols in this category are the "products" of the "transformed consciousness," they are also regarded as working to "transform" the human being in its entirety.

Continued on next page

were, that ultimately leads to conversion. This dynamic of revelation is uniquely transformative. Dulles makes this explicitly clear when he notes that:

> A symbol . . . communicates by inviting people to participate in its own meaning, to inhabit the world which it opens up, and thereby to discover new horizons, with new values and new goals. Symbols do something to us. They shift our center of awareness and thereby change our perspectives and values. Symbols, therefore, have the kind of transformative power that is needed for conversion to come about. Without symbols, no revelation could be effectively communicated.[159]

This has been developed above, in sections "Transformative Effects" and "Insights into Mysteries" of this chapter.

[159]Dulles, *The Craft of Theology,* 65. See also Dulles, "Revelation and Discovery," 4, 10-13, especially 4 and 11. Dulles points out that "discovery is an insight that changes the knower's outlook or horizons." Moreover, "discovery begins with a state of mind called wonder." The individual considers the "data" that is part of his or her experience and considers that which is "beyond" the borders of this experience. This arouses curiosity, questioning, and, eventually searching. See also Dulles, *The Assurance of Things Hoped For,* 215: "Faith, then, is initially achieved by a mysterious process of discovery in which the human mind, impelled by grace, lights upon a truth beyond all that it could logically derive from the data of common experience."

Revelation, the self-disclosure of the divine presence (which is already "gift"), offers boundary experiences that challenge the recipient to go beyond the framework of existence that has become familiar. These boundaries lie not only within the life of the individual but, more specifically, in the presuppositions of faith and experiences of God held by the individual. These boundaries, when experienced and "pushed," create new horizons of knowledge, understanding, awareness, and even real experiences of the divine self, that will, in turn, be transformative for the individual.[160] Yet, true Christian conversion or transformation never happens in isolation. If the transformative effects of revelation are to take root in the life of the individual, he or she must be a member of a community of faith. Once again the "community" is the locus for experience *and* transformation.

-----

[160]See Dulles, "Revelation and Discovery," 20-24, especially 20. Dulles addresses Rahner's notion of the "self-transcending movement" and the relationship between revelation and discovery. This discussion deals with the idea that "if Christian theologians could point to nothing more than disclosure experiences, there would be little to distinguish them from those who reject the concept of revelation, . . . [those] who write simply of 'limit experiences' . . . or 'peak experiences'." Dulles contends that "disclosure" can be, at the same time discovery and revelation. "It would be discovery insofar as it was a fulfillment of a human heuristic craving and revelation insofar as the fulfillment was a gift of God."

Knowledge and Understanding Realized

The acknowledgment of the rightful and significant place of community in the process of divine self-disclosure (the locus for experience *and* transformation) flows from an understanding of the foundational elements of the community. These elements, the *active* life of faith and the *tradition* of the community (understood to be the "history of the community's lived experience of God and action of faith"[161]), form the crucible in which knowledge and understanding of God, and the experience of the divine presence take place.

Throughout this work we have argued that the "symbolic theory" holds that revelation cannot take place apart from the symbols by which it is mediated. Some symbols are understood to be the fundamental historical and biblical symbols of the Christian faith; these are the "primary" symbols. Other symbols are characterized by the attributes of the community of faith through which they flow—that is to say, in which they are generated or "created;" these are the "secondary" symbols. If they are to realize their revelatory possibilities, the secondary symbols must be easily recognized and have a cognitive impact on the members of the community. If the language used is not

---

[161]See Dulles, "Faith and Revelation," 120-123. See also Dulles, *The Craft of Theology,* 87-104, especially 94-98 where Dulles summarizes *DV,* chapter 2, on tradition. The notion of tradition will be dealt with extensively in the next chapter.

familiar to the one who is to receive that which is being communicated, reception will not take place. Consequently, the symbols must resonate with the experience of a particular community in search of the divine self-presence.

Moreover because of the "cognitive content implicit in the originative symbols, revelatory symbolism is able not only to 'give rise to thought' but also to shape the thought it arouses."[162] Dulles goes on to point out that,

> authors such as Rahner, in their theology of revelation, speak paradoxically of "mediated immediacy." This term aptly conveys the dualism of the explicit and the implicit, the thematic and the unthematic, the datum and the horizon in any revelatory experience. *What is immediate, for Rahner, is the self-communication of the divine, the experience of grace. But the inner presence of God cannot be known and cannot achieve itself except insofar as it becomes mediated, or mediates itself, in created symbols. The symbols, however, do arouse a genuine awareness of the divine itself—an awareness that always surpasses all that we can say about it.*[163]

---

[162]Dulles, *Models of Revelation*, 144. Cf. Dulles, "The Symbolic Structure of Revelation," 62.

[163]Dulles, *Models of Revelation*, 148-149. Cf. Dulles, "The Symbolic Structure of Revelation," 69-70. Our emphasis. Dulles uses the phrase "authors such as Rahner . . ." in many places throughout his development of "Symbolic Realism" and "Symbolic

Continued on next page

Symbols "give rise to thought," "shape the thought [they] arouse," mediate the "immediacy (the self-communication of the divine, the experience of grace)," and arouse the "awareness of the divine." In other words, symbols possess a heuristic element that "sparks" the human psyche into a spiritual struggle, as it were, between the "thematic and the unthematic."[164]

Mediation." It is evident that Rahner continues to be a profound influential force on Dulles' thought.

[164]W. M. Urban, *Language and Reality* (London: Allen & Unwin, 1939), 415. "The peculiar character of insight symbols lies in the fact that they do not point to or lead to, but they lead *into;* . . . they are, or at least are supposed to be, a vehicle or medium of insight."

The language Dulles uses to speak of the elements that are in dialectic tension (the "spiritual struggle"), namely, the "unthematic" and the "thematic" is clearly borrowed from Rahner. Rahner speaks of *Vorgriff,* which is derived from the German compound verb *vorgreifen; vor* - before and *greifen* - to grasp; hence, literally translated, "before grasped" (*griff* being the preterit form of the verb). The term implies the concept that we know something about a reality without being "consciously" aware of the reality itself—that is to say, "before" it is "grasped." In other words, it is the "known unknown." Rahner uses an example of the sun and colors. We know something of the sun (without seeing it) simply by virtue of our ability to see colors. The concept of discovery, for Dulles, is the process of grasping the not-yet-known. See Dulles, "Revelation and Discovery," 9, 13, 20.

Dulles also speaks of this concept in terms of "anticipatory knowledge (*Vorgriff*) of God [which] is a coefficient of all human awareness." See Dulles, "Faith, Church and God," 539-540. See also Rahner, *Foundations of Christian Faith*, 318-321. With discovery comes an existential awareness of God; in the process of discovery
Continued on next page

It is becoming clear that symbols have a much more important relationship to cognitive knowledge than one might suspect at first glance. In applying the theory of "symbolic realism" to the "cultural-linguistic" category of doctrine developed by George Lindbeck, Dulles insists that "symbols have greater cognitive importance" here.

> They are signs imbued with a plenitude or depth of meaning that surpasses the capacities of conceptual thinking and propositional speech. A symbol, in this perspective, is a perceptible sign that evokes a realization of that which surpasses ordinary objective cognition. Symbolic knowledge is self-involving, for the symbol "speaks to us only insofar as it lures us to situate ourselves mentally within the universe of meaning and value which it opens up to us."[165]

Adhering to a recognition of the cognitive element of symbol calls into clear focus the possibility of knowledge, not just *about* God, but also *of* God's essence. This is not to say, however, that

we move from "knowing something of God before we are able to come to some 'thematic' awareness," to an "existential awareness" and experience of God. *Vorgriff*, then, is an expression that deals with that which is present before we are aware of it. It is, so to speak, the unthematic horizon.

[165]Dulles, *The Craft of Theology*, 18-19. Dulles is quoting himself as found in *Models of Revelation*, 136. See also Dulles,

Continued on next page

revelation, symbolic communication and knowledge, is to be understood "as an insertion of fully formulated divine truths into the continuum of human knowledge but rather as the process by which God, working within human history and human tradition, enables his spiritual creatures to discern more profoundly the true meaning of their existence;"[166] a meaning that offers insight and knowledge of God's essence in relationship to humanity.

In his elucidation of symbolic mediation, Dulles offers two examples, parable and ritual, as characteristic of the actual expression of this "symbolic mediation." Dulles introduces the first example through the work of Norman Perrin.

> Parables, according to Norman Perrin, can function either as similes or as metaphors. If the parable is a simile, it "teases the mind into recognition of new aspects of reality," often by using symbols or myths, such as, in the parables of Jesus, the Kingdom of God. If the parable is metaphorical, it "produces a shock which induces a new vision or world and new possibilities . . . for the experiencing of that existential reality which the myth mediates."[167]

"Revelation and Discovery," 20-22. See also Lindbeck, "Dulles on Method," 53-62.

[166]Dulles, "Revelation and Discovery," 21.

[167]Norman Perrin, *Jesus and the Language of the Kingdom*, (Philadelphia: Fortress, 1976), 202 as quoted by Avery Dulles, *Models of Revelation*, 134.

Dulles also points out that "many of the biblical parables are primarily oriented toward evoking a decision, but they contain symbolic elements which serve to mediate revelation."[168] In other words, the biblical parables are, for the most part, transformative in nature, calling the person or the community to new horizons and ways of orienting their lives. These symbolic elements are the basis through which knowledge and understanding arise. They bring forth a new vision, as it were, while offering, cognitive "information" about the divine presence.[169]

The second example Dulles cites is that of ritual. He defines ritual as a "symbolic or mythic narrative in action." He goes on to say that:

> [Ritual] dramatically renews the sacred events which it recalls. By participation in the ritual the worshipper is able to discern ultimate meaning, to

---

[168]Dulles, *Models of Revelation*, 134.

[169]See, for example, O'Collins, *Retrieving Fundamental Theology*, 103: "The double-sided way . . . symbols function [as 'symbols of the times,' articulating the situation of one's current context of life, and as symbols that 're-present' invisible realities and communicate religious meaning] obviously makes them suitable vehicles for God's *revealing and saving* self-communication. Symbols have a cognitive content and always say something . . . All communicate some truth and transmit some information. At the same time, we can never hope to express conceptually once and for all the meaning and truth of these symbols."

integrate the negative elements of existence, and to experience the power of the sacred.[170]

Ritual, if it is to be understood as "symbolic or mythic narrative in action," *is* the very narrative of the community. The ritual becomes a unique and particular expression of the cognitive content of the activity of God's presence in the community's midst. This *narrative* is formed and shaped by the community's collective experience of, and testimony to, the self-disclosure of God. The narrative, through ritual, then serves the community as its on-going source of information for education and formation. To "discern ultimate meaning," therefore, is to gain access to knowledge of these narrative events in and through the events of the sacred ritual.

How does one *know* if the revelation is *actually* of God? Might it not simply be something created in the dysfunctional psyche of an individual or the mass hysteria of a "spiritual" gathering of people? With the cognitive elements of symbol duly noted, it is important to round out this exposé of Dulles' theory of symbolic realism and the symbolically mediated self-

---

[170]Dulles, *Models of Revelation,* 134. See especially Dulles, "Faith, Church, and God," 541: the "collective consciousness of the community;" 545: "a reestablishment of continuity within its own history as a group." See also Dulles, *The Communication of Faith and Its Content,* 15-16; "Faith and Revelation," 122: "The liturgy is the place where many of the faithful most vividly experience the saving mysteries and prayerfully reflect on the *contents* of their faith." Our emphasis.

disclosure of the divine by addressing, in more detail, his understanding of the reception of revelation (characterized *only* within the parameters of a community of faith and not along isolated, individualized lines), and the truth of the content of this revelation.

Reception and Knowledge of Revelation

A fundamental notion that is significant for Dulles (in his paradigm of symbolic realism) has been suggested in various places throughout this exploration of the symbolic context of revelation. Nevertheless, it must be rearticulated here. It is certainly true that,

> no clear dichotomy can be drawn between the symbolic and the nonsymbolic. [Moreover,] all *comprehension* demands that we go out of ourselves and *dwell in* the subsidiaries in order to perceive their joint meaning. *But in symbolic knowledge a deeper degree of indwelling is required.* To enter the world of meaning opened up by the symbol we must give ourselves; *we must be not detached observers but engaged participants.*[171]

---

[171]Dulles, *Models of Revelation,* 132-133. Our emphasis.

These notions of "indwelling" and "participation" continue to surface, time and time again, in the theology of Dulles. These two factors are essential for reception and full knowledge of divine revelation. We will begin by addressing "indwelling."

Indwelling

As we have already indicated, Dulles' use of the notion of "indwelling" derives, in part, from Michael Polanyi's discussion of the "personal [active] participation of the knower in what he knows."[172] This notion of indwelling is basic to Dulles' paradigm of symbolic realism. His method is to "reflect on the process by which the original tacit knowledge of revelation arises. It comes about, in [Dulles'] opinion, through a form of communication which [he] calls symbolic."[173] It is

---

[172]We refer the reader to Chapter Two of this work, specifically footnotes 72 and 80. See also Dulles, *A Church to Believe In*, 48.

[173]Dulles, *Models of Revelation*, xix. It is important to point out here, that there appears to be a difference, a "reversal" of sorts, in Dulles' appropriation of the work of Polanyi with regards to the "universal" and the "particular" aspects of the notion of tacit knowledge. According to Polanyi we comprehend an entity by *attending to* its particulars. We have a "subsidiary" awareness of the "proximal term," in the process of tacit knowing, by attending to the "distal term." Polanyi uses the example of electric-shock therapy. The subject who experiences electric shock is able to draw a "connection between" the experience of the shock (the "distal term") and the conditions surrounding the experience of the shock

Continued on next page

important for Dulles that the symbolic communication that mediates this revelation finds a grounding in the "dwelling in" of the symbols. Both the individual believer and the community of faith participate in this process. Dulles believes that by "dwelling in" the symbols that mediate the self-communication of God, human beings come not only to experience the presence of the divine, but also to embrace an identity uniquely framed by God's own self-disclosure.

(the "proximal term"). Polanyi states that this connection is "tacit" because the subject's attention is focused on the shock producing "particulars." Tacit knowing, then, involves a relationship between the universal and the particular, or in Polanyi's words, the "proximal term" and the "distal term." See Polanyi, *The Tacit Dimension,* 6-10, 13, especially 8-9.

Dulles, however, seems to invert this concept. Dulles maintains that it is the comprehensive reality of revelation, as such (the "distal term") and not particulars (for him, the "models" of revelation - or the "proximal term") of which we have tacit knowledge. Moreover, it is, for Dulles, a process of "attending to" the specific, or the particular, models that flow "from" our tacit knowledge of revelation. ". . . One apprehends the clues in a subsidiary or tacit manner and concentrates on their joint meaning." See Dulles, *The Craft of Theology,* 9. See also *Models of Revelation,* 258. See also the section on "Participatory Knowledge" in Chapter Two of this work, especially note 72.

In short, the "reversal" lies in the fact that for Polanyi we "attend from" the "proximal term" to the "distal term," whereas, for Dulles, we "attend to" the "proximal term" (the models of revelation) from the "distal term" (revelation, itself). See Polanyi and Prosch, *Meaning,* Chapter Four.

The new identity is one that each Christian shares with others. It is the corporate identity of the Christian community, into which the individual is integrated as an extension of his or her own self. Christians see and hear no longer with their own eyes and ears alone, but with those of the Church to which they now belong. They think its thoughts, and it thinks in them. Their faith is a participation in the faith of the Church, to which they submit as the rule of their own believing. They know what the community knows, not with mere spectator knowledge, whereby one gazes at something, but by an inner familiarity, through *indwelling,* somewhat as we know our own bodies. The more completely the believer *dwells* in the community of faith and relies upon it, the more lively will be his or her sense of the Christian faith, and the better will he or she be able to see the deficiencies in the ways that Christians have previously expressed their faith, and the more creative they will be in adapting Christian doctrine and symbolism to new and unprecedented situations. Paradoxically, commitment to the Church is a normal prerequisite for competently criticizing the Church.[174]

---

[174]Dulles, *The Craft of Theology*, 66. Our emphasis. In this particular section, Dulles is speaking about Christian conversion in the case of converts to the faith. We would suggest that it also seems to possess general significance for all members of the Christian community and not just new converts.

Continued on next page

Consequently, for Dulles indwelling involves not only the symbols that mediate the revelation but also the community within which the revelation is communicated. A dynamic interchange exists between the symbols and the symbolic

---

See also Augustine, *De Praedestinatione Sanctorum 2:5 (Patrologia Latina*, ed. Migne, 44:963): "No one believes anything without first thinking that it ought to be believed."

See also Dulles, "Faith, Church, and God," especially 545-546. Here Dulles addresses one of the few religious themes that Polanyi explores—namely, worship and ritual. "Celebration or ritual, [Polanyi] held, is an essential feature of any community. It educates the feelings of the members, draws the members into deeper communion, and thus enhances their life together." See also Dulles, *Models of Revelation,* 144.

See especially, Lindbeck, *The Nature of Doctrine*, 35. Lindbeck is here speaking about the "requirements" to become "religious" according to the cultural-linguistic schema. ". . . To become religious—no less than to become culturally or linguistically competent—is to interiorize a set of skills by practice and training. One learns how to feel, act, and think in conformity with a religious tradition that is, in its inner structure, far richer and more subtle than can be explicitly articulated." Dulles recognizes that this "interiorization" is concomitant with "indwelling."

Terrence Merrigan, in his article "Models in the Theology of Avery Dulles: A Critical Analysis," *Bijdragen, Tijdschrift voor filosofie en theologie,* 54 (1993), 141-161, raises a caution regarding the notion of "indwelling" in Dulles. Merrigan (p. 156) suggests that " . . . Dulles does not seem to countenance the possibility of fallibility as far as the knowledge acquired by 'indwelling' is concerned." The following section, *"Sensus Fidelium,"* will address the topic of the "fallibilty" of indwelling.

language that communicate the revelation and the individual believer within his or her community of faith.

To articulate the process of indwelling is to acknowledge the fact that "to apprehend its true meaning, one must *pass through* the symbol to what it makes present (re-presents)." As Kelly notes, however, "this is true to an extent of all types of communication, even the indicative signs of ordinary language."[175] Nevertheless, in contrast with the indicative signs of ordinary communication, there is a significantly greater and fundamentally deeper degree of indwelling with the real symbols that are "utilized" for revelation. This results from the very

---

[175]Kelly, "Knowing by Heart," 69. Kelly uses an image similar to the one that Dulles utilizes in *The Communication of Faith and Its Content*. Kelly goes on to say that "to read a text . . . one must pass through the printed shapes of the letters to grasp the words and the meanings for which they stand. Still further, one passes through individual words to comprehend their joint meaning in sentences and paragraphs; finally, one may sense and come into contact with the author's mind and outlook expressed in a whole essay or book. Such comprehension is already symbolic, and involves a measure of participation."

See Dulles, *The Communication of Faith and Its Content*, 8: "The symbolic approach operates with a triadic view of knowledge. The *subject* is seen as dynamically tending to achieve a religious *meaning* by integrating *clues* afforded by experience. The three irreducibly distinct elements are the subject, the clues, and the meaning." In other words, the person of faith must "dwell in," or "pass through" the clues to come to "know" what meaning is contained and communicated. See also Dulles, "The Symbolic Structure of Revelation," 60-61.

nature of this particular symbolic language—language that, unlike "ordinary" communication, re-presents the self-disclosure of the divine.

Moreover, (and this recalls the "transformative" and "insight" elements of symbolism), we find ourselves open to,

> enter into a relationship with the reality expressed in the symbols in a way that requires a greater surrender of intellectual control . . . One learns from the symbol what it means, instead of allowing one's prior knowledge to dictate to it what it must (and must not) mean.[176]

Our relationship to reality, therefore, is guided, influenced, and transformed by the very symbolic language that mediates God's self-disclosure. This, in turn, allows us the opportunity for greater perception and awareness of that revelation.

Dulles' notion of indwelling is crucial for his discussion of "symbolic knowledge." This knowledge is the truth, as it were, that is garnered from the very act of reception and indwelling by the community of faith—reception of the revelation of God's self. Dulles makes this quite clear when he writes that,

> symbolic knowledge . . . is here used to include a wide spectrum of figurative or nonliteral

---

[176]Kelly, "Knowing by Heart," 70.

communication, whether by word or by deed. Symbols, by their evocative power, arouse the imagination and *invite participation*. As contrasted with literal discourse, symbol induces a kind of *indwelling* in the world of meaning to which it points. Symbols frequently make known a meaning too deep or comprehensive for clear articulation; they arouse *tacit awareness* of things too vast, subtle, or complex to be grasped in an explicit way; they bridge contrasts that defy conceptual integration.[177]

In short, symbols provide believers with a profound "sense" of the faith. Moreover, the sense of the faith of the individual becomes an enriching part of the collective experience of the faith of the community. In turn, the community offers the locus for the validation of the interpretation of the "primary" symbols and the re-definition of the "created" symbols that articulate the divine self-expression. This validation is the *sensus fidelium,* or the "sense of the faithful." It is evident that the second most significant element in the schema of Dulles is keenly linked to the first.

---

[177]Dulles, *Models of Revelation*, 257. Our emphasis. See also Dulles, *The Assurance of Things Hoped For*, 214-218, especially, 214: " . . . it would seem that informal or tacit reasoning plays a greater role than formal reasoning in the approach to faith."

Sensus Fidelium[178]

The "*sensus fidelium*" has been described as "the implicit or prepredicative, communal 'knowledge' of the faith acquired through immersion in the revelatory tradition."[179] Dulles equates it with what John Henry Newman called— in the case of the individual—the "illative sense." Dulles describes the "illative sense" as "the personal power [natural reasoning power sharpened by experience] to discern and assess the force of multiple convergent signs that could not be turned into logical

---

[178]See John Henry Newman, *On Consulting the Faithful in Matters of Doctrine,* ed. John Coulson (London: Collins Liturgical Publications, 1961). See also Terrence Merrigan, *Clear Heads and Holy Hearts: The Religious and Theological Ideal of John Henry Newman,* Louvain Theological & Pastoral Monographs, 7 (Louvain: Peeters Press, W. B. Eerdmans, 1991), especially 202-228.

[179]Merrigan, "Models in the Theology of Avery Dulles," 151. Merrigan offers this definition during his discussion of the problem of the "assessment" of "models" in the methodology of Dulles: "Dulles' approach to the problem of assessment or evaluation is fundamentally the same and consists in an appeal to what is best described, in 'classical' theological terminology, as the *sensus fidelium*."

See also Dulles, *The Craft of Theology,* 9, 12. See Dulles, "Faith and Revelation," 120-123, especially 121. See also Lindbeck, *The Nature of Doctrine,* especially 35, and his understanding of what it means to become "religious" within the cultural-linguistic schema. See Thomas Hughson, "Dulles and Aquinas on Revelation," *The Thomist,* 52 (1988), 445-471.

premises."[180] The essence of the illative sense lies in its being an "acquired" wisdom, insight, and knowledge. It is acquired through experience; experience, in this context, of the community of faith. It is through participation in the lived experience of the divine presence in the community that one acquires "tacit or implicit knowledge" of the divine.[181] This knowledge, though

---

[180]Dulles, *A Church to Believe In,* 42. See also Dulles, *Models of Revelation*, 258.

[181]See Dulles, *Models of Revelation*, viii: "All Christian believers, it could be said, tacitly know what revelation is simply by virtue of adherence to a revealed religion. But they do not yet have a formulated concept or theory of revelation."

Polanyi's notion of "indwelling," which is a constitutive factor in his epistemology and analysis of "tacit knowledge" appears to be, for Dulles, parallel with Newman's notions of "implicit reasoning" and the "illative sense," which make up the epistemological framework of "*sensus fidelium.*" See also Dulles, "Faith, Church, and God," 538: Dulles writes that "at this point Polanyi the scientist speaks, probably without realizing it, in almost the same terms as Newman the theologian." Compare Polanyi, *The Tacit Dimension,* and *Personal Knowledge*, with Newman, *On Consulting the Faithful in Matters of Doctrine* and *An Essay in Aid of a Grammar of Assent* (Garden City: Doubleday Image Book, 1955).

More specifically, for Newman, "revelation always involves a dimension of tacit awareness[;] its contents can never be clearly and comprehensively spelled out." See Dulles, "From Images to Truth," 255. Moreover, the coming to this "tacit awareness" is garnered only in participation in the life, and tradition, of the community of faith.

Furthermore, it is also important to note that "for Newman, Scripture is one of the principal media, and in some sense

Continued on next page

implicit, offers the believer a certitude on which a judgment for assent can be made.

> By *participation* in the community of faith the individual believer can have reliable access to the revelatory meaning of the signs and symbols through which God's self disclosure has taken place and through which God's salvific designs have been made known. Through these signs and symbols believers can *more fully grasp* God's revelation than they could through the use of unaided reason.[182]

That the community plays a significant role in the *interpretation and understanding* of the symbols and symbolic language that function as the medium for God's self disclosure should be obvious. The community, both its tradition and the active

---

the primary medium, through which the revealed idea comes to the believer, but it is not the sole medium." See "From Images to Truth," 258. However, the "revealed idea" cannot be gained without the help of and the adherence to the tradition. It becomes the balancing factor, as it were. We will return to an exploration of Scripture and Tradition, and their respective relationship to revelation and Dulles' enterprise in the following chapter.

Merrigan, however, suggests that there is a "greater isomorphism" between Newman and Dulles than between Polanyi and Dulles. See Merrigan, "Models in the Theology of Avery Dulles," 156, 161.

[182]Dulles, "Faith and Revelation," 98. Our emphasis.

expression of the faith of its members, is the key to the "sense" of the faith.

A challenge, perhaps even a caution, can be leveled against this understanding of revelation as symbolically mediated. This challenge considers the possibility of a "lack of a cognitive element" in revelation because of its "symbolic nature" and its tendency toward "tacit knowledge." However, though it may be understood that,

> . . . symbolic knowledge is evocative, and that it appeals more to tacit than to explicit reason, . . . symbolism is not on that account noncognitive, still less irrational. Revelation, although it cannot be verified by deductive or empirical tests, can be validated by criteria of the kind that are applied to other forms of symbolic knowledge.[183]

---

[183] Dulles, *Models of Revelation*, 271. Dulles mentions that when revelation is verified and validated by the criterion of symbolic knowledge, it "prove[s] possible to forge a viable path between the opposite extremes of rationalism, which would insist on formal demonstration, and fideism, which would seek to dispense with all rational grounds of credibility." See *Models of Revelation,* 258-259, especially 259.

We should not confuse Dulles' understanding of the criteria utilized in the verification of revelation with the criteria he identifies for the assessment of particular "models" of revelation. Dulles points out "seven" criteria for judging the validity of, or assessing, theories of revelation. They are as follows: [1] faithfulness to the Bible and Christian Tradition; [2] internal coherence; [3] plausibility; [4] adequacy to experience; [5] practical
Continued on next page

The most important criterion of validation, here, is Newman's notion of the *sensus fidelium.* "Acceptance of revelation is achieved and manifested within a living community of faith in which the insights of all the members are exchanged and subjected to mutual criticism, so that illusions can be detected and exposed."[184]

---

fruitfulness; [6] theoretical fruitfulness; [7] value for dialogue. See *Models of Revelation,* 17. Merrigan points out that "Dulles retains these seven criteria [the criteria used in the assessment of models of the church] but conflates rootedness in Scripture and tradition, and the promotion of corporate identity and Christian values. At the same time, he adds two new criteria, namely, 'internal coherence' and 'plausibility,' by which he means that theories of revelation must be 'free from internal contradiction' and compatible with 'what is generally thought to be true in other areas of life.'" See Merrigan, "Models in the Theology of Avery Dulles," 149. Our *inclusio.* Dulles writes that the criteria are possessed of only "limited utility." See Dulles, *The Craft of Theology,* 49; See Dulles, *The Assurance of Things Hoped For*, 214-218.

[184]Dulles, *Models of Revelation,* 259. Dulles notes that in view of the ambiguity of some symbols and the possibility of misinterpretation, it is to be understood that *participation in* the faith community is that which offers "definiteness" to the symbolic language. See especially, *Models of Revelation*, 144. Symbols must be interpreted within the structures and faith experience of the community. In other words, it is a constant dialogue of faith, an "engagement," as it were, with the symbols and with each other so that the "truth" and the "definiteness" of the revelation can be drawn out.

See also O'Collins, *Retrieving Fundamental Theology*, 106: O'Collins asks the question: "But what makes symbols credible?"
Continued on next page

An element we have yet to address involves what constitutes the essence of community—that is to say, the constitutive element that characterizes and identifies it as a "community of faith," one capable of reception and knowledge of divine self-disclosure. This element is, in a phrase, a shared "fund of tacit knowledge," and, by extension, a shared "fund of tacit meaning."[185] This "fund of tacit knowledge" becomes the

---

He answers that, to some extent, "historical evidence . . . the history of someone or some event is essential for determining the meaning and truth of some symbols. But finally it is personal experience that legitimates the symbolic realities, especially those which make up the Christian message and life. Lived symbols are believable symbols. By appropriating and entering into the central symbolic realities of Christianity, we allow them to 'veri-fy' themselves or make themselves true. We validate experientially symbolic knowledge, in particular the symbolic knowledge of faith." The validation, experientially, takes place within the community of faith. He goes on: "Our remembered and shared symbols identify and define the Christian community. They allow us to receive God's salvific self-communication, to communicate with each other and to hand on our faith in Christ to the next generation."

[185]Dulles, *Models of Revelation,* 116-117, especially 128. Dulles also identifies this as "a certain prethematic awareness of the reality of revelation [that] is given to all in faith." It is only through this, properly understood, that a theology of revelation can surface.

What is significant here is that the "fund" of knowledge and meaning is "shared." The importance of this is seen when Dulles clarifies Newman's understanding that "no revelation can be complete and systematic . . ." Dulles writes that, "in other words, the mysteriousness of the divine grows in direct proportion, and

Continued on next page

vehicle through which the process of the discovery of the reality
of revelation takes place. The fund of tacit meaning offers itself
as the material element for the expression and articulation of the
reality of God's self-disclosure. "Revelation is, in principle, an
apprehension in which the mind rests satisfied. Faith, however,
is a stretching forth of the mind toward an insight not yet given,
or not clearly given . . . Faith sustains the process of
discovery."[186] In other words, "meaning" and comprehension can
come to the surface only through fervent analysis of the symbols
and symbolic language that are the medium for this shared fund
of knowledge and discovery. Even so, Dulles asks the question:
How is reason involved in this disclosure process?

> The discernment is not an achievement of formal
> or explicit reasoning, such as takes place in
> mathematical or syllogistic logic. Revelatory
> knowledge rests on the tacit integration of clues
> which to conventional thought might appear
> disconnected and incoherent. By arousing the
> imagination, the affections, and the heuristic
> impulses, symbols initiate and direct a process

---

not in inverse proportion, to the completeness of revelation." See
Dulles, "From Images to Truth," 257.

See also Dulles, "Revelation and Discovery," 9, 10-11, 20,
especially 26-27, 28; *The Communication of Faith and Its Content,*
14-15; *A Church to Believe In,* 42-46.

[186]Dulles, *Models of Revelation,* 280. Cf. Dulles,
"Revelation and Discovery," 25.

whereby the mind, relying partly on unspecifiable clues, perceives radically new patterns and meaning in particular constellations of data. If such tacit inference is ranged under the heading of reason—as Newman and Polanyi would wish it to be—we may properly claim that the transmission of revelation through symbol involves the use of reason. Even so, the moment of illumination is an unexpected gift that comes when it will. Theologically speaking, the discernment of revelation is a grace.[187]

The symbolic process of revelation is, therefore, necessarily and intimately connected to the community of faith. That which cannot be empirically verified can find validation within the experience of the community. It becomes confirmed (and verified) when it "rings true"—that is to say, when the members of the community experience conversion, a conversion that brings about new insights and understandings and, in turn, has an impact on their behaviors and commitments. Revelation is recognized as truth when it is seen, as such, through the

---

[187]Dulles, *Models of Revelation,* 258. See also Polanyi, "Faith and Reason," 237-247, especially 247: "The discoverer works in the belief that his labors will prepare his mind for receiving a truth from sources over which he has no control." In Dulles' words: ". . .The moment of illumination . . . [happens] when it will." See also Dulles, "Revelation and Discovery," 1-29, especially 2, 20. The very "discernment of revelation" is a "grace."

"corporate judgments of the total community of faith,"[188] the sense of the "faithful."

Christ as the Symbolic Whole of God's Self–Disclosure

Dulles maintains that "religions are characterized—and distinguished from one another—by their symbols."[189] We have seen that, within his notion of symbolic realism, Dulles understands symbols to be influenced by Christian convictions and positions of faith. This stance of faith is, at the same time, an openness to the symbols that mediate God's revelation. Furthermore, the very meaning of being "influenced by Christian convictions" bespeaks the symbols' rootedness in the Judeo-Christian faith—the Bible and the *living* tradition of the community of faith. More specifically, articulated in the language of symbolic realism, Dulles contends that,

> . . . if a symbol is understood (following Karl
> Rahner) as the self-expression of one reality in

---

[188]Dulles, *Models of Revelation,* 259. Dulles writes: "If we know more than we can say, and if we know tacitly more than we know explicitly, it should not be surprising that in matters of personal faith the evidences should sometimes be of a sort that cannot be marshaled for forensic debate." See also Dulles, "Faith and Revelation," 109. See Dulles, *The Assurance of Things Hoped For*, 172: "By means of symbols and metaphors the mind often attains to truth that eludes direct declarative statement."

[189]Dulles, *The Communication of Faith and Its Content*, 6.

another, distinct from it yet one with it, then
Jesus' behavior [during his public ministry] . . . is
[readily identifiable as] a symbol. So [also, and] in
a larger sense, is the New Testament itself, and
the whole revelation of God in the Scriptures and
in the Church. In them all, a graced awareness of
who God is finds tangible expression in human
and finite forms. Only in this way—only through
symbols, in other words—can this reality "get
through to us" without ceasing to be *God's*
reality.[190]

---

[190]Kelly, "Knowing by Heart." 64. Kelly also offers an
overview of Dulles' thought. He intends to show, more concretely,
how revelation is to be understood as symbolic. He also intends to
identify a "psychological model for understanding the process of
revelation; . . . to describe what happens in a certain typical
disclosure situations—the manifesting of an otherwise hidden divine
meaning."

See especially, Rahner, *"Zur Theologie des Symbols,"* 292.
["The Theology of the Symbol," 236]: ". . . The Father is himself
by the very fact that he opposes to himself the image which is of
the same essence as himself, as the person who is other than
himself; and so he possesses himself. But this means that the Logos
is the 'symbol' of the Father, in the very sense which we have
given the word: the inward symbol which remains distinct from
what is symbolized, which is constituted by what is symbolized,
where what is symbolized expresses itself and possesses itself."

Furthermore ". . . The incarnate word is absolute symbol of
God in the world, filled as nothing else can be with what is
symbolized. He is not merely the presence and revelation of what
God is in himself. He is also the expressive presence of what—or
rather, who—God wished to be, in free grace, to the world, in such a
way that this divine attitude, once so expressed, can never be
Continued on next page

In other words, the full expression of who God is, the self-manifestation of the divine, must be symbolically mediated—interwoven with the constructs of human history—in order for human beings to come to know God and "God's reality."

Nevertheless, "these symbols do not operate in isolation, but they mutually condition and illuminate one another. Christianity, therefore, cannot be reduced to a single symbol, even that of Jesus Christ. The Christ-symbol does not function *except* in the context of the Old Testament background and the response of the Christian community, fundamentally presented to us in the New Testament."[191] Dulles does not, however, move away from identifying Christ as the "summit" of revelation.

---

reversed, but is and remains final and unsurpassable." See *"Zur Theologie des Symbols,"* 293-294. ["The Theology of the Symbol," 237.]

And finally, "it follows from what has been said [above] that the Logos, as Son of the Father, is truly, in his humanity as such, the revelatory symbol in which the Father enunciates himself, in this Son, to the world—revelatory, because the symbol renders present what is revealed." See *"Zur Theologie des Symbols,"* 296. ["The Theology of the Symbol," 239.] Our *inclusio*.

[191]Dulles, *The Craft of Theology*, 19; see also 26-28. Our emphasis. Cf. Dulles, *The Communication of Faith and Its Content*, 6-7, 9.

Dulles also raises the question of whether the "symbolic approach" could lead to a doctrine of revelation "in which Christ is not longer uniquely normative, but is reduced to 'one symbol among others'?" He comments that some theologians and philosophers of religion have "moved in that direction." He offers some considerations of this question in "Christ the Summit of

Continued on next page

If revelation is understood as symbolic communication, the primacy of Christ is not difficult to grasp. The divine Son, the Word of God, is symbolically present and active in Christ's human nature, which becomes a medium through which the divine manifests itself. For us who do not immediately encounter Christ in his incarnate life, his character and meaning have to be mediated by proclamation, Scriptures, liturgy, and sacraments, and only to the extent that this mediation is successful does Christ become for us the fullness of revelation. But if the mediation is successful, Christ does appear as a uniquely powerful and unsurpassable revelation of God. His life in the flesh, together with his message of forgiveness, supremely manifests what God chooses to be in free grace toward human kind. In Christ's wonderful deeds, especially his miracles, God's kingdom may be seen breaking into the history of the world. The crucifixion, as a symbolic event, expresses the sacrificial character of God's redemptive love. The resurrection symbolizes, by its very reality, the victory of that redemptive love over all that could oppose it, even hatred and death. Without Christ we could not come to know and respond to God as the one

---

Revelation," Chapter 10 of *Models of Revelation*, dealing with Christology. See also Cook, "Revelation As Metaphoric Process," 401-411.

who "so loved the world that he gave his only Son" (John 3: 16).[192]

---

[192]Dulles, "Faith and Revelation," 99. See also *GS* 10, 44; *LG*, 8; *DV*, especially 4.

Furthermore, "the Catholic Church has always looked upon Jesus Christ as the supreme self-communication of God. Lateran Council IV (1215) gathered up the sense of many new Testament passages when it declared that Jesus Christ as the Incarnate word manifested the way of life with special clarity (*viam vitae manifestius demonstravit,* DS 801). The Council of Trent (1546) spoke of the gospel as the source of all saving truth and moral discipline (*fontem omnis et salutaris veritatis et morum disciplinae,* DS 1501). The same council solemnly taught that the gospel is transmitted through Scripture and apostolic Traditions. Vatican Council I (1870) repeated in substance the teaching of Trent on Scripture and Tradition, but made significant advances by its pronouncements on revelation, faith, and the magisterium. Not only did Vatican I detail the ways in which revelation is communicated to the faithful in the Church, it also spoke eloquently of the Catholic Church as a sign raised up among the nations, inviting them to come to faith and at the same time confirming the faith of its own members. (DS 3013-3014)." See Dulles, "Vatican II and Communications," in *Vatican II: Assessment and Perspectives, Twenty-Five Years After (1962-1987),* 3 vols. ed. René Latourelle (Mahwah: Paulist Press, 1988), 3:529.

Dulles, however, is aware of the problem in today's pluralist world that "the modern mind, deeply impressed by the limitations imposed by the particularities of time and culture, has difficulty in admitting that there can be any absolute or unsurpassable disclosure within history." See also Dulles, "Faith and Revelation," 101. Dulles refers to the fact that, because of these concerns, Vatican II avoided the formula associated with revelation, namely, that it "ceased with the death of the last apostle." He points out, on the same page, that, "on at least two occasions, the Theological

Continued on next page

Kelly offers further clarification. He insists that "Jesus *gives* that revelation [the self-disclosure of God] insofar as he makes the connection explicit for his hearers [specifically in parables and healings]; [further] he first *receives* [this] revelation insofar as he sees the connection—that is, allows it to be made in him."[193]

Once again, we see that revelatory symbols are linked intimately with "communication"—verbal and non-verbal—in the revelatory act. This becomes apparent in the life of Jesus, the medium by which God communicates the God-self to humanity. Kelly goes on to explain that,

---

Commission or its subcommissions rejected several *modi* requesting that *Dei Verbum*, no. 4, be amended to state explicitly that revelation was closed (*clausam*) with the death of the apostles. See the *relationes* of July 3, 1964, and November 20, 1964. These are found respectively in the *Acta Synodalia Sacrosancti Concilii Oecumenici Vaticani II,* Periodus 3, vol. 3 (1974), and Periodus 4, vol. 1 (1976), p. 345." *DV* instead describes Jesus as the perfecter and fulfillment of revelation and claims that "the Christian dispensation, therefore, as the new and definitive covenant, will never pass away, and we await no further public revelation before the glorious manifestation of our Lord Jesus Christ (see 1 Tim. 6:14 and Tit. 2:13)." See *DV* 4.

[193]Kelly, "Knowing by Heart," 78. Here, Kelly cites Rahner who observes that "the theology of the process of the act of faith and that of the revelation-occurrence are to a large extent identical." See Karl Rahner, "Revelation," in Karl Rahner and Joseph Ratzinger, *Revelation and Tradition,* translation by W. J. O'Hara (New York: Herder and Herder, 1966), 19.

the revelation or message, therefore, does not preexist the symbol that conveys it, as if the latter were a wholly indifferent, external channel. Instead, it emerges into full clarity in the act of being told. Its language and imagery, its narrative structure, even its historical context are intrinsic to the revelation itself. So too the person and life history of Jesus are intrinsic to what he reveals, belong to what make him the perfect and final revelation of God.[194]

---

[194]Kelly, "Knowing by Heart," 78. See also Dulles, *Models of Revelation,* 267: "[Dulles] would insist on the profound affinity between the symbolic and the historical approaches to revelation. The symbols of biblical and Christian faith, while they build on certain cosmic archetypes, are enriched and further specified through the historical memories of ancient Israel. Persons standing within this tradition have solid reasons for doubting that God reveals Himself with equal fullness to those who are unfamiliar with that history. Why should God not have expressed Himself most distinctly through a given strand of human events? To hold on principle that God **must** be equally accessible through the experience of every people, or through the common symbolism of nature and consciousness, would be as groundless as to hold that the mind of an artist must be equally manifest in everything that this artist produces, or that a total stranger can know a person as well as a close friend or relative can. According to the biblical and Christian view, God is best known through those deeds of love by which He has manifested Himself in the history of Israel and in the career of Jesus. Inasmuch as Jesus is the Incarnate Word, his humanity is something more than a representative symbol. Rather, it is a *presentative* symbol—one in which the God who is

Continued on next page

That throughout Christian history Jesus has been seen
and held to be "the perfect and final" revelation of God does not
mean that God is no longer active in the process of self-
disclosure to humanity. Dulles points out that "Vatican Council
II, while insisting on the permanence of the covenant established
in Christ, recognized that God is not silent in our time."[195] In one
sense this can be understood in the context of revelation as
"simultaneously revealed and hidden." Dulles insists, that in
particular sections of *Lumen Gentium* and *Dei Verbum*, a
profound attempt was made to "avoid giving the impression that
the church already possesses a *total grasp* of revelation in its
fullness, but at the same time they emphasize the Church's

---

symbolized is present and operative, somewhat as a human person
is present in the body and its gestures."

See Dulles, "The Symbolic Structure of Revelation," 67-68.
In Dulles's own footnote to this material he points out that "my
term 'presentative symbol' corresponds approximately to what
Karl Rahner has called 'symbolic reality' (*Realsymbol*) as distinct
from 'symbolic representation' (*Vertretungssymbol*). Cf. Rahner,
"*Zur Theologie des Symbols*," 279, 290. ["The Theology of the
Symbol," 225, 234.] Cf. also Liberatore, "Symbols in Rahner," 148.

[195]Dulles, "Faith and Revelation," 102-103. He offers
several quotations to illustrate his point: *DV 21, 8* (Not only
Scripture, but also tradition, is seen as the locus of continuing
revelation); *SC 7* (The liturgy is expressive of the multiple
presence of Christ in the church); and *GS 11, 4* (The signs of the
times as indications of "God's presence and purpose in the
happenings, needs, and desires in which this people [the church] has
a part along with other people of our age").

obligation to adhere faithfully to 'the mystery of the Lord,' the 'Christian dispensation,' the 'new and definitive covenant'."[196]

In an attempt to offer some concluding comments on Dulles' conception of the symbolic structure of revelation it seems appropriate to highlight some of his closing remarks in the 1980 article that served as a springboard into this theological enterprise.

> The symbolic or sacramental structure of revelation is impressively, though very concisely, indicated in Vatican II's Constitution *Dei Verbum*. Revelation is seen as a loving approach whereby God mysteriously emerges from His silence and invites His beloved creatures to enter into fellowship with Himself. "This plan of revelation is realized by deed and words having an inner unity: the deeds wrought by God in the history of salvation manifest and confirm the teaching and realities signified by the words, while the words proclaim the deeds and clarify the mystery contained in them." The fullness of revelation is not a vocal or written word, but Christ himself, who "is both the Mediator and at the same time the fullness of all revelation." God makes Himself known through the sign of a human existence which refers itself totally to the divine person who possesses it as His very own.

---

[196]Dulles, "Faith and Revelation," 101-102. See also O'Collins, *Retrieving Fundamental Theology,* 100.

> Thus revelation, as imparted through Jesus
> Christ, has a symbolic structure. It may suitably
> be described as symbolic disclosure.[197]

This symbolic disclosure has become for Dulles, a decisively fruitful way to embrace and explore the self-communication of God. This schema allows him to call the Church to a deeper awareness of itself, its relationship to God, and, in turn, its relationship to the world.

For Dulles, then, that revelation is symbolically mediated is self-evident. The human being can only come to an awareness and comprehension of revelation through symbol; the human being is held to be symbolic in nature. Revelation, by its very nature, the self-disclosure of the divine, is itself symbolic. It is a shared process—that is to say, a process involving a dynamic commitment to an intimate relationship on the part of God and on the part of the human being, as an individual in community. Revelation is also shared from another perspective, in that it cannot, and will not, take place without the initiative of God and the openness and willingness to actively seek the Divine on the part of human beings. Therefore,

> the true content of revelation—revelation in the
> objective sense—is the divinely intended and
> humanly perceived significance of the events and

---

[197]Dulles, "The Symbolic Structure of Revelation," 73. See also *DV*, 2.

words. By *participation in the community* of faith
the individual believer can have *reliable access* to
the revelatory meaning of the signs and symbols
through which God's self-disclosure has taken
place and through which God's salvific designs
have been made known. Through these signs and
symbols believers can more fully grasp God's
revelation than they could through the use of
unaided reason.[198]

We now have to turn our attention to the effects and the
consequences, the responsibilities and the requirements, that this
"participation" in the ecclesial community requires from its
members. The ecclesial community will be, henceforth, the
necessary point of departure for a fuller "grasp" of God's self-
disclosure.

---

[198]Dulles, "Faith and Revelation," 98. Our emphasis.

CHAPTER FOUR
DULLES AND AN ECCLESIAL-TRANSFORMATIVE APPROACH TO REVELATION

An Ecclesial-Transformative Doctrine of Revelation

A Redefinition of Lindbeck's "Cultural-Linguistic" Category

The apparent crystallization of Avery Dulles' more recent theological work is found, rather poignantly, in his re-working and appropriation of Lindbeck's "cultural-linguistic" framework.[199] Most simply understood, "ecclesial transformative" theology may be equated with Dulles' notion of "symbolic realism"—most specifically, with the *transformative*

---

[199]The reader is referred back to Chapter One, the section entitled, "The Cultural-Linguistic Theory of Doctrine," especially footnote 33.

elements of symbol and symbolism. Dulles' renaming the category also bespeaks his central conviction that the *experience* of the *community* of faith (*ecclesia*) forms the locus for understanding the self-communication of God as symbolic mediation.

As we have seen, participation in the experience of the community becomes the source and substance of the individual's appropriation and apprehension of the very symbols that mediate the revelation of God. This experience is by definition (or necessity) a shared experience. Not only do individuals "share" it with others—that is to say, with all members of the community—but the community itself "shares" an experience of the divine with its tradition—that is, with the historically grounded experience of the communities that have gone before it, all "marked with the sign of faith." In other words, the community offers a distinctive setting through which the saving and redeeming realities of God's self-communication may be experienced. Again, revelation, for Dulles, is,

> regarded as a real and efficacious self-communication of God, the transcendent mystery, to the believing community. The deeper insights of revelatory knowledge are imparted, not in the first instance through propositional

discourse, but through participation in the life and worship of the church.[200]

Consequently, he maintains that the primary content of faith, the "subject matter," as it were, of the "ecclesial-transformative approach," is the "saving self-communication of God through the symbolic events and words of Scripture, especially in Jesus Christ as the 'mediator and fullness of all revelation.'"[201] Imparted through the life and worship of the church, these symbolic events "come alive," so to speak, and become living realities that mediate God's presence in their midst.

Furthermore, Dulles argues that, through dwelling in these revelatory symbols and dwelling in the community, the individual of faith comes not only to experience the divine presence, but also to realize an identity that is uniquely

---

[200]Dulles, *The Craft of Theology*, 18. We have noted earlier that Dulles points out the observation by Lindbeck that to become religious "is to interiorize a set of skills by practice and training. One learns how to feel, act, and think in conformity with a religious tradition that is, in its inner structure, far richer and more subtle than can be explicitly articulated." See Lindbeck, *The Nature of Doctrine,* 35. The reader is referred back to Chapter One, especially footnote 32. Cf. Dulles, "Vatican II and the Recovery of Tradition," in *The Reshaping of Catholicism: Current Challenges in the Theology of Church* (New York: Harper and Row, 1988), 75-92. See especially, 83-86. ["*Das II. Vatikanum und die Wiedergewinnung der Tradition" In Glaube im Prozess: Christsein nach dem II. Vatikanum - Für Karl Rahner*, 546-562. See especially, 553-557.]

[201]Dulles, *The Craft of Theology*, 19. *DV, 2*.

characterized by God's self-disclosure. This identity, although "taken on" as a result of an assent of faith, is an on-going process of awareness and understanding. In turn, it contains two distinctive elements which are both processes unto themselves. These two elements are intertwined. They do not occur in isolation, but radically affect each other, calling forth commitment and challenge, conversion and growth.

The first of these elements is the process of "socialization" and the formation of the members of the community—including, most especially, the neophytes. Dulles suggests that "we know the community to which we belong not by looking at it from outside but by dwelling in it and merging our own existence into its collective life. The formation of adult members occurs through a process of socialization."[202] The second element is the process of "traditioning"—that is to say, the on-going articulation and expression of the faith and experience of the divine presence in the midst of the community. "Faith is an interpretation of clues or symbols. Such an interpretation is an art and has the structure of a skill. Skills . . . are not normally acquired by individuals in isolation, nor are they learned out of books. Skills are transmitted by proficient persons in an atmosphere of personal trust."[203] This "atmosphere of

---

[202]Dulles, *The Communication of Faith and Its Content*, 15. See also Dulles, *The Craft of Theology,* 66.
[203]Dulles, *The Communication of Faith and Its Content*, 14. See also Dulles, "Discovery and Revelation," 25-29, especially 25-
Continued on next page

personal trust" *is* the community of faith. The "transmission of skills," broadly understood, may be identified with the "transmission of the faith," or, the process of "traditioning." These two elements are indicative of the "ecclesial-transformative" approach to revelation and, more broadly, theology.[204]

A Process of "Socialization"—The Individual

As we have noted before, there are two kinds of knowledge—namely, objective knowledge (knowledge by empirical, scientific examination) and tacit knowledge (knowledge

---

26 and Polanyi's notion of "apprenticeship." See also Polanyi, *Personal Knowledge*, 53.

[204]See Dulles, *The Craft of Theology*, 20-21: Dulles maintains that the human being is "socially and historically constituted." He holds that, as historical beings, people "achieve the benefits of culture [read=community of faith] by *appropriating the insights of their forebears*, as these insights are transmitted in the cultural heritage [read=traditioning]." Moreover, "the assimilation of social and historical symbols requires *readiness to open oneself to the ideas and values that these symbols embody* [read=socialization process]." He goes on to say that "faith is not just an act of the intellect but a transformation of the whole person in response to God's initiatives, conveyed through the religious community and its tradition." Our emphasis and *inclusiones*. See Dulles, *The Assurance of Things Hoped For*, 215.

by instinct or connaturality).[205] Tacit knowledge is a knowledge that is "located" not only "in the mind" but also in the very being of the individual. In a sense, from a corporeal perspective, this type of knowledge could be termed "muscle memory." The knowledge is tacitly in the "muscle" of the body itself. When typing on a keyboard one does not necessarily "think" about which key he/she needs to strike; instead, the person's fingers, hand and arm muscles, in conjunction with each other, "know" which keys to strike. Dulles highlights other examples such as swimming, bicycling and playing the piano. He maintains that: "I [Dulles] know more than I can say, even to myself. To actuate my knowledge, I must perform, and in the very performance I can seize my knowledge, as it were, in action."[206] The individual may, in a very real sense, "know" how to do these particular things, but explaining them in an articulate way so that someone else may "grasp" the knowledge is quite a bit more difficult. Dulles suggests that the knowledge can be "grasped" and "articulated" only through the very "doing" of the action, through its "performance."

Dulles recognizes the fact that this experience is similar to the knowledge a person of faith has in considerations of faith.

---

[205]We refer the reader back to Chapter Two, the section entitled "Communication and the Transmission of Symbol."

[206]Dulles, "Vatican II and the Recovery of Tradition," 84. ["*Das II. Vatikanum und die Wiedergewinnung der Tradition,*" 554-555.]

"The church and its members know the God of Jesus Christ by a kind of personal familiarity, by dwelling in the faith. Faith-knowledge is, in the first instance, tacit. It is a kind of instinct or second nature that prompts us to worship and to behave as believers do."[207] The "exact words" or the "exact way" or the "exact knowledge" for discovering God, for example, can not be imparted. The "skill [however] can be imparted by the experience of being affiliated to a community of faith . . . Christian faith is ordinarily acquired by living within the church and participating in its corporate life."[208]

In the first instance, this participation in the corporate life of the community, more specifically, the Catholic Christian community, finds expression most clearly in its ritual and worship.

> A privileged locus for the apprehension of this subject matter is the worship of the Church, in which the biblical and traditional symbols are proclaimed and 're-presented' in ways that call for active participation (at least in mind and heart) on the part of the congregation. The interplay of symbols in community worship arouses and

---

[207]Dulles, "Vatican II and the Recovery of Tradition," 84. ["*Das II. Vatikanum und die Wiedergewinnung der Tradition,*" 554-555.]
    [208]Dulles, "Vatican II and the Recovery of Tradition," 84. ["*Das II. Vatikanum und die Wiedergewinnung der Tradition,*" 554-555.]

> directs the worshipers' tacit powers of apprehension so as to instill a personal familiarity with the Christian mysteries.[209]

Personal familiarity becomes, in turn, an experience of conversion and transformation. The believer engages, and is engaged by, the revelatory symbols and the shared dynamic of the experience of the community. The believer comes to a deeper awareness of the transcendent Reality and, accordingly, a deeper awareness of self and one's relationship to the created world. This engagement and awareness re-creates the individual, so to speak, in the very mysteries of the faith.

---

[209]Dulles, *The Craft of Theology,* 19. Cf. Dulles, *The Communication of Faith and Its Content,* 15. In this work Dulles speaks of liturgy as a "school" in which a "living sense of the faith takes root."

See also Dulles, *The Craft of Theology,* Chapter 4, entitled "Fundamental Theology and the Dynamics of Conversion," 53-68, especially 66 where Dulles writes: ". . . No Christian conversion is complete unless it situates the convert solidly within the community of faith." This chapter distinctly addresses both types of "conversion:" conversion of the individual along with the ecclesial dimension of conversion.

For an excellent exposition on tradition and creativity, see also Dulles, "Tradition and Creativity: A Theological Approach," in *The Quadrilog: Essays in Honor of George H. Tavard,* ed. Kenneth Hagan (Collegeville: The Liturgical Press/A Michael Glazier Book, 1994), 312-327, especially 323 as it correlates with the line of thought in this section.

Kelly's reflection on Dulles' enterprise offers some clarity. He suggests that,

> the symbols of faith, therefore, not only reveal the mystery of God, but in so doing reveal believers to themselves, as persons oriented to the mystery. This brings with it the invitation—and obligation—for them to commit themselves in freedom to the mystery and to that which reveals it: to affirm it, to rely on it, to recreate its presence continually so that its influence can permeate their lives.[210]

What is most essential here is the notion of an "invitation and obligation" flowing from the revealed mystery of God. This invitation and obligation extends over time as an on-going commitment to place one's self at the depths of the transcendent

---

[210]Kelly, "Knowing by Heart," 82. Kelly observes, in the same place, that ". . . faith requires one to let oneself go, in trust and love, to what is beyond oneself; in drawing me out of myself, the signs of faith reveal to me my own transcendence. When I believe, I put myself consciously and freely at the disposal of that over which I have no control, trusting in a wisdom and a goodness greater than my own. The supreme expression of such faith is found in the final words of Jesus on the cross: 'Into your hands I commit my spirit'."

See also Dulles, *Models of Revelation*, 219. Dulles speaks of the ongoing process of revelation. The revelation of God continues in and through the faith of the community. Dulles observes that without the church as a presentative symbol, "we would not be able to know Christ as he really is."

mystery, through the symbols of faith. Consequently, conversion and transformation become a perpetual experience in one's life.

The question remains, How does this process take place? Is it simply a matter of joining a community of faith? Does its expression consist solely in participating in a community's liturgical life? How are the "skills" of interpretation actually passed on? What is necessary for this on-going commitment? What are the requirements? Dulles finds an answer, once again, in the work and musings of Michael Polanyi. Dulles takes off from Polanyi and suggests that as the scientist must be "apprenticed," so too, must a member of a community of faith (whether they be a new convert or a life member) be "apprenticed"—that is to say, submit to the education and environment of the community.[211]

The symbolic dimension of reality is inherent to the ecclesial-transformative framework. Dulles maintains that, in this context, faith is an interpretation of and assent to the symbols that characterize a particular religious tradition and which are expressed and experienced in the life of the individual and the community. Moreover, he suggests that the process of

---

[211]Dulles, "Vatican II and the Recovery of Tradition," 81. [*"Das II. Vatikanum und die Wiedergewinnung der Tradition,"* 551-552.] See also Dulles, *The Communication of Faith and Its Content,* 14-15; "Discovery and Revelation," 25-29, especially 25-26 and Polanyi's notion of "apprenticeship;" "Tradition and Creativity," 322. See also Polanyi, *Personal Knowledge,* 53.

interpretation that is implicit in a stance of faith is itself an "art and has the structure of a skill." He goes on to say that,

> skills—whether in economics, medicine, carpentry, the fine arts, or religion, to give only a few examples—are not normally acquired by individuals in isolation, nor are they learned out of books. Skills are transmitted by proficient persons in an atmosphere of personal trust. The neophyte must willingly submit to education within a community that values the skill and under the guidance of masters who can impart it.[212]

This is not only for the neophyte. The handing on of skills is a continuing shared process of experience for all the members of the community. Once a skill has been passed on, the recipient knows how to do some particular thing. But, of course, it always is possible to develop the skill—that is to say, to participate in the process of perfecting it. This sort of growth and development is a life-long process in the believer's quest for and

---

[212]Dulles, *The Communication of Faith and Its Content*, 14. See also Dulles, "Revelation and Discovery," 26: "To become a violinist, an actor, or a painter is possible only through a prolonged period of apprenticeship in which the master imparts to the disciple the techniques [read=skills] and methods of creative performance." With faith, the community and its shared experience of the divine self-communication becomes the master. See also Dulles, "Faith, Church, and God," 540-546, especially, 540-541.

discovery of God. It is a process of "traditioning"—specifically, a "process of 'traditioning' the faith." As such, it "include[s] practically everything that the church does,"[213] for this traditioning is the work of the community.

"Traditioning"[214] *and the Ecclesia—The Community*

"Christian tradition is in the first instance the handing on from generation to generation of what is tacitly known by the community."[215] As we have just noted, this "handing on" process is the key factor in the socialization, formation, and transformation of individual believers. Dulles suggests that the process of traditioning provides an integral and interactive connection between the community of faith and the individual believer. The connection involves a vested interest, a commitment, on behalf of both parties. It becomes a relationship

---

[213]Dulles, "Faith and Revelation," 121.

[214]The notion of "traditioning" will surface again in a following section. There the distinction will be made between "Tradition," "traditioning," and "traditions." The three "facets" are an integrated whole describing the "revelation" of God in the lived experience of the community of faith.

[215]Dulles, "Vatican II and the Recovery of Tradition," 86. [*"Das II. Vatikanum und die Wiedergewinnung der Tradition,* 556.] See also Dulles, *Models of Revelation*, 50. Dulles quotes Michael Polanyi, who observes that "a society which wants to preserve a fund of personal knowledge must submit to tradition." See Polanyi, *Personal Knowledge*, 53.

of, on the one hand, searching and questioning (by the individual believer), and on the other hand, being willing to struggle with and share the common fund of faith (by the community). This is not to say that the community has all the answers. But traditioning does require a willingness to enter into a dialogue-of-faith, so that insight and collective truth surface through dialogue.

This process is, obviously, not peculiar to the ecclesial-transformative approach. Traditioning has been, at least implicitly, understood as an on-going process throughout the centuries. Dulles offers three significant ways through which the church has taught, either "informally or implicitly," in this process of "traditioning"—namely, through its life of worship, through the writings of the fathers, and through the sense of the faithful.[216]

Dulles accurately notes that throughout the centuries the Christian community has recognized, and attempted to live by, a vital relationship between *lex orandi* and *lex credendi*. He points out that, in the liturgy, "many of the faithful most vividly experience saving mysteries and prayerfully reflect on contents of their faith."[217] Thus the community's life of worship itself

---

[216]Dulles, "Faith and Revelation," 121-123.

[217]Dulles, "Faith and Revelation," 122; "Faith, Church, and God," 545-546; "Revelation and Discovery," 11, 23-24, 28; "Vatican II and the Recovery of Tradition," 86. [*"Das II. Vatikanum und die Wiedergewinnung der Tradition,* 556-557.]; *The Craft of Theology* [Expanded Edition, 1995], 210. Dulles points out the links between worship and dogma while exploring the maxim

Continued on next page

becomes a form of traditioning. So too, the writings of the fathers, exceptional witnesses to the tradition of the Christian community, "writers of Christian antiquity distinguished for sanctity and orthodoxy,"[218] function as a form of traditioning asserted by the church. Dulles points out the church's recognition of the close connection between the theology of the fathers and their life of prayer and worship. He notes the "providential role" these writers played in the establishment of the canon of Scriptures, the creed, and basic dogmas, as well as their contribution to the basic structure of the church itself and its liturgy.[219] What is most notable is that while the fathers were, in the past, "agents" of the process of passing on the tradition and the transmission of revelation, their agency is itself a continuing process—through their writings and their accomplishments. "The transmission of this revelation is not a static repetition, but an ongoing reexpression and resymbolization. The unfolding of Christian faith through the early centuries, from the New Testament era to the time of the great church councils, shows this process at work."[220] Finally,

---

lex orandi/lex credendi. He states that this maxim "needs to be put to work in both directions. We must interpret the liturgy in the light of the declared faith of the Church, and we must contemplate the dogmatic inheritance as an outgrowth of the Church's corporate worship."

[218]Dulles, "Faith and Revelation," 122.

[219]Dulles, "Faith and Revelation," 122.

the "sense of the faithful" functions as a third form of traditioning. We have covered this topic in detail in the previous chapter. What is important to emphasize here is that "life within the church as the body of Christ has a profound influence on the ways in which people feel and think. The Holy Spirit, animating the church, produces in faithful members an instinctive sense of what agrees or disagrees with revelation."[221] Animated by the

---

[220]Kelly, "Knowing by Heart," 80. Kelly goes on to explain the "process:" "What Jesus announced as the coming reign of God is resymbolized in the first disciples' proclaiming him as risen and as Lord. The apostle Paul reexpresses the good news in ways that appeal to his increasingly gentile audience, in the process helping transform the Christian movement from a Jewish sect into a world religion. Later still, the Fourth Gospel radically transposes themes from the synoptic tradition in its narrative reinterpretation of Jesus' life and message. The early Christian creeds attempt to formulate the contents of Christian belief, leading in time to the patristic theologies and the conciliar definitions that express that faith in terms very remote from the world of first-century Judaism." See, "Knowing by Heart," 80.

Kelly goes on: "Underlying these repeated transformations, nevertheless, is a process at least analogous to that which brought the original revelation into being. I [Kelly] have suggested that when Jesus utters a parable (for instance), his tacit knowledge of God, operating through imagination, 'gives itself a body'. . .The knowledge conveyed only comes to be, fully, in the symbol that embodies it."

[221]Dulles, "Faith and Revelation," 122. See also William M. Thompson, *"Sensus Fidelium* and Infallibility," *American Ecclesiastical Review* 167 (1973), 450-86. See also Jean M. R. Tillard, *"Sensus Fidelium,"* *One in Christ* 11 (1975), 2-29.

Continued on next page

Holy Spirit, this instinctive sense is the very life pulse in the community's quest for God. "Tradition itself is not grasped by objective knowledge—that is to say, by looking at it—but by participatory knowledge—that is, by dwelling in it."[222]

Although the process of traditioning is not unique to the ecclesial-transformative approach, this approach is distinctive in that it sees the community as well as the individual as a locus of transformation. In *The Craft of Theology* Dulles maintains that the ecclesial-transformative approach to revelation and theology "may be able to shed some light on many traditional questions."[223] In this way, it may specifically illuminate the transformative aspect as it affects the *ecclesia* and not just the individual believer. Insights into theological questions and the revelatory symbols that are expressive of the faith offer "a building up of the church," as it were, with a deeper embrace and an enrichment of that which places the community in an environment to apprehend the transcendent reality of God's self-communication. According to Dulles,

---

For an in-depth exploration of the theme of the "sense of the faithful," see the classic work by John Henry Newman, *On Consulting the Faithful in Matters of Doctrine.*

[222]Dulles, "Vatican II and the Recovery of Tradition," 86. [*"Das II Vatikanum und die Wiedergewinnung der Tradition,"* 556.]

[223]Dulles, *The Craft of Theology,* 26.

revelation is not complete without the Church. If there were no community of believers, revelation as a transaction would be cut short. For revelation, as a communication from God to human beings, destined for their conversion and redemption, achieves itself only when it is received and responded to in faith.[224]

Hence, the response in faith effects the actualization of conversion that flows out of the experience and, in turn, becomes an on-going call for further conversion and transformation.

What becomes evident from our discussion is an awareness of the "energizing life" inherent in the experience of faith. Once articulated and shared, the self-disclosure of the divine finds its full grounding in the very heart and essence of the life of the community. Dulles believes that,

revelation, which reaches its term in the interior act whereby it is believed, spontaneously comes to expression in a bodily and social manner through external acts of confession. It achieves a public and historical existence when the testimony of the first witnesses becomes constitutive of an enduring community of faith. For the testimony to evoke the response of faith it must be both humanly credible and divinely fructified by the assistance of the Holy Spirit,

---

[224]Dulles, *Models of Revelation,* 220.

172 • Symbolic Mediation

> who moves the witnesses to give *testimony* and at
> the same time *enlightens* the minds of the hearers.
> The mediation of revelation, therefore, is not a
> purely natural process but one that depends on
> God's continuing activity.[225]

In other words, the community, as it provides a window into the
mysteries of God for its members, inspires them to offer their
own testimony of faith. And, as Dulles rightly points out, the
entire process is rooted in a trust and hope in God's continued
activity in the world and in loving relationship to the world.

Dulles offers some comments by way of summarizing his
understanding of the process of traditioning. He observes that,

> the essential and primary function of Christian
> tradition [read=the process of traditioning] is not
> to transmit explicit knowledge, which can better

---

[225]Dulles, "Faith and Revelation," 117. Our emphasis. In a
footnote for this section Dulles points out that some theologians
indicate this, the connection between the mediation of revelation
and God's continuing activity, through the terms "dependent" or
"repetitive" revelation. He writes: "The theme of *dependent
revelation* was proposed by Paul Tillich in his *Systematic Theology*
(Chicago: University of Chicago Press, 1951), 1:126-28, and has
been taken up in contemporary Catholic theology by Gerald
O'Collins (*Fundamental Theology* [New York: Paulist, 1981], 100-
102), among others. The term *repetitive revelation* was used by the
Anglican John Macquarrie in his *Principles of Christian Theology*
(New York: Scribner's, 1968), 80-81, 93." See "Faith and
Revelation," 117.

be done by written documents, nor simply to provide a method of discovery, but to impart a tacit, lived awareness of the God to whom the Christian Scriptures and symbols point.[226]

For those who espouse and maintain an ecclesial-transformative approach to revelation (understood as the symbolic communication of the divine self), the role of the community is quite clear. It functions as the animating force behind the tacit, lived awareness of God, assisting in the interpretation of the revelatory symbols. Dulles suggests that some of the most powerful of such symbols are found within the Christian Scriptures. Scripture, intimately linked to tradition as the "one source and font" of revelation, and yet linked in another sense to the teaching authority of the Church, will be our final point of exploration.

Scripture, Tradition, Magisterium

Catholicism provides a distinct perspective for these considerations of the transmission of divine revelation. Catholic theology maintains a doctrine of tradition as a divinely authoritative norm to be used in conjunction with the sacred Scriptures. Moreover, viewed from the ecclesial-transformative

---

[226]Dulles, "Vatican II and the Recovery of Tradition," 86. [*"Das II. Vatikanum und die Wiedergewinnung der Tradition,"* 557-557.]

framework set up by Dulles, Scripture and tradition are
intertwined sources of revelatory symbol. They demand a
faithful interpretation by the "masters" who are capable of
passing on to the members of the community the skills that lead
to insight into the divine presence. Dulles, drawing from the
Dogmatic Constitution on Divine Revelation, asserts that this
role is played by the "living teaching authority of the church."
Dulles posits that,

> Scripture, tradition and the magisterium are
> inseparable and mutually interdependent (DV 10).
> Since the three are reciprocally coinherent, no one
> of them can be used as a totally independent
> source to judge or validate the other two.
> Theologically, Scripture has no normative value
> except as read in the light of tradition and under
> the vigilance of the magisterium. Tradition and the
> magisterium, conversely, have no value except as
> referred to Scripture.[227]

---

[227]Dulles, *The Craft of Theology*, 98. The "living teaching
authority of the church," officially understood as the magisterium,
is regarded as endowed with a special responsibility for the passing
on of the faith and the interpretation of revelation through sacred
scripture and tradition. There is some discussion as to the
possibility that the "living teaching authority of the church" may
also include theologians. Certainly they are the "working hands" of
the magisterium and play a significant role. See, for example,
United States Bishops Committee, "Doctrinal Responsibilities:
Approaches to Promoting Cooperation and Resolving
Misunderstandings between Bishops and Theologians," *Origins 19*

Continued on next page

As we round out our reflections on the ecclesial-transformative approach to revelation and theology, it makes sense to consider these three elements individually.

The Sacred Scriptures

In one sense, we have already reflected on the Scriptures within the ecclesial-transformative framework. Dulles maintains that biblical language speaks quite clearly, and is symbolically representative, of the self-communication of the divine and its

---

(1989), 97-110. See also Congregation for the Doctrine of the Faith, "Instruction on the Ecclesial Vocation of the Theologian," *Origins 20* (1990), 117-126.

Dulles points out that "tensions can arise between the hierarchical authorities and the theologians." He goes on to say: "From some literature one gets the impression that the two groups are engaged in a perpetual contest, and that every advance of one group is achieved at the expense of the other." See Dulles, *The Craft of Theology*, 106. What of the broader picture, however, i.e., the bigger discussion of the shared faith and the sense of the faithful? Dulles' falling back on the magisterium seems also to suggest that there may be a tendency to slip into, at times, a cognitive-propositional approach. We will raise this as a concern in the next section.

The exchange between Philip and the Ethiopian eunuch in Acts of the Apostles 8: 26-40, suggests some biblical support for this understanding. Philip asks the eunuch: "Do you really grasp what you are reading?" The eunuch replies: "How can I unless someone explains it to me?"

attendant transformative effects. The symbols found in the scriptural texts serve not only to mediate the revelation of the divine, but also to create an implicit awareness of the existential reality of God that exists in the life of the community. Like many other theologians, Dulles holds "that the revelatory power of the Bible is diminished if one does not allow the stories to work in a symbolic way on the reader's affections and imagination."[228] When it becomes linked explicitly to tradition, however, Scripture plays a more substantial and fundamental role in Dulles' thought.

> The emerging ecclesial-transformative theology takes a mediating position [with regard to Scripture and tradition as 'sources of' revelation]. It looks to Scripture and tradition *both* as expressing the faith of the original community and as shaping the faith of subsequent generations. The two 'sources' in combination transmit the message less by explicit statement than by forming the imagination and affectivity of the Christian community. The biblical and traditional symbols impart a tacit, lived awareness of the God who has manifested himself of old. By appropriating the symbols and 'dwelling in' their meaning, new [and old] believers are able to apprehend reality, as it were, through the eyes of their predecessors in the faith. Scripture and

---

[228]Dulles, *The Craft of Theology*, 82.

tradition are instruments through which God, who spoke of old, continues to address the believing community today.[229]

Scripture and tradition create the environment in which the community of faith exists. This environment embraces the believer, situating him or her in a context through which the

---

[229]Dulles, *The Craft of Theology,* 23. Our *inclusio* and emphasis. Dulles cites *DV,* 8 and 21. He also makes reference to Chapter 12 of his *Models of Revelation.* He cites Chapters 5 and 6 of his *The Craft of Theology* as further reference.

It is also important to note that, implied in this quote [yet only against the background of Dulles' entire schema], is a multitude of other important facets. Although the text specifically addresses "new believers," it would appear to hold true for "current" members of the community. Through the process of "indwelling," as we have noted above, all members "grow in awareness" and come to a deeper understanding of the reality of God's self-communication.

Furthermore, as Dulles points out, Scripture and tradition are both involved in *"expressing* the faith of the original community and . . . *shaping* the faith of subsequent generations." This understanding is significant in that it indicates the continuing "transformation" of both the individual of faith *and* the community of faith.

Moreover, though it is not explicitly mentioned, Dulles explores this area as an "inseparable" element in the discussion of Scripture and tradition. He addresses it in detail in Chapter 7 of *The Craft of Theology.* The magisterium plays a significant role in the "formation of" and guidance in "apprehension" of the reality of God. It is the "authoritative judge of the conformity of particular doctrines and practices, including human traditions, with the word of God." Cf. Dulles, *The Craft of Theology,* 104.

presence of God can be realized. This is an environment of faith-in-question that assists and nurtures its members in their own process of discovering God. Furthermore, in and through the process of individual discovery, the community also grows. It comes to incorporate new expressions and articulations of the reality of the transcendent and immanent God in its midst.

It is important to clarify Dulles' use of the language of "sources" in his above discussion of Scripture and tradition. Despite his intentional use of the word (the quotation marks are his qualifier), Dulles rightly understands that Scripture and tradition flow from "one source"—the divine self-disclosure of God. In one of the six points of summary that he offers in a reflection on the second chapter of *Dei Verbum,* "The Transmission of Divine Revelation," Dulles speaks of the relationship between Scripture and tradition. He points out that, in *Dei Verbum* 7, these two elements constitute a "single mirror" through which the pilgrim church contemplates God. "They derive from one wellspring (*scaturrigo*)—a term that recalls the statement of Trent that the gospel is the one source (*fons*) of all saving truth (DV 9; Cf. DS 1501)."[230] Moreover, "Vatican II

---

[230]Dulles, *The Craft of Theology*, 96. Dulles' other points of summary on *Dei Verbum* will surface shortly. We mention one other point here: *"The problem of distorting tradition."* Although the question of "distorted tradition" surfaced at the Council (namely by Cardinal Meyer), Dulles points out that the council "nowhere describes Scripture as a norm for validating tradition, but its teaching on the authority of Scripture implies that nothing
Continued on next page

accepts the idea, affirmed in Vatican I, that the word of God exists in a twofold form: as canonical Scripture and as tradition. Scripture is the *verbum Dei scriptum;* tradition is the *verbum Dei traditum* (DV 10; Cf. DS 3011)."[231]

In some more recent theological musings, the classical phrasing of "scripture and tradition" has given way to a clearer articulation of the tandem relationship of these two "sources" of revelation. The expression in current use, "Scripture **in** tradition,"[232] more accurately conveys the interconnectedness of these two key "sources." Scripture *in* tradition bespeaks not only their interdependent relationship but also the historical conditioning that is necessarily a part of the "formulation of the canon." The Scriptures cannot be viewed apart from the tradition out of which they were formulated, in which they were codified, and through which they offer a symbolic mediation of the divine presence for contemporary believers. Tradition is needed, as it

contrary to God's word in Scripture could have any claim to be authentic tradition." See, The Craft of Theology, 97.

[231] Dulles, *The Craft of Theology*, 96.

[232] David Tracy, "On Reading the Scriptures Theologically," in *Theology and Dialogue: Essays in Conversation with George Lindbeck,* ed. Bruce D. Marshall (Notre Dame: University of Notre Dame Press, 1990), 37-38. Tracy maintains that "this 'Scripture in tradition' principle continues . . . to be the most fruitful theological one for assessing the central role of Scripture for Christian theology as the plain *ecclesial* sense." Tracy is aware of the fact that Lindbeck, about whom he is writing, does not explicitly use this phrase, but he substantiates its attribution to Lindbeck in a footnote.

were, in order for the community of faith to have a foundational structure within which to grasp the word of God. This is said, of course, against the backdrop of the recognition that the church regards all revelation as contained in Scripture.[233]

Tradition, tradition and traditions[234]

Since the Second Vatican Council, a distinction has often been made in common theological parlance (purely for abstract discussion purposes), between "the *Tradition,* (with a capital T) [understood] as *the* revealed message, *tradition* as a process of transmission ('traditioning'), and *traditions* as diverse forms of expression of the gospel."[235] The revealed message, *Tradition,* is

---

[233] An issue that will not be taken up in this thesis, yet is at least pointed to by Dulles, involves the question as to whether tradition contains any revealed truth not present in Scripture.

[234] For a detailed consideration of *Dei Verbum,* see O'Collins, *Retrieving Fundamental Theology,* 48-62, 136-149. For an extensive bibliography on *Dei Verbum* see also, Appendix 2, 178-217. See also the authoritative commentary on the document by Joseph Ratzinger in *Commentary on the Documents of Vatican II,* ed. Herbert Vorgrimler (New York: Herder and Herder, 1969), 3:181-198.

[235] Dulles points out that "apologists for the council took over from the Montreal report on 'Scripture, Tradition, and the Traditions,' (no. 39) this distinction." See Dulles, *The Craft of Theology,* 100-102. See also, *The Fourth World Conference on Faith and Order, Montreal 1963,* Faith and Order papers 42, ed. Patrick C. Rodger and Lukas Vischer (London: SCM; New York: Association, 1964).

Continued on next page

the principal reference point of this thesis. The specific expressions of the gospels and the early Christian communities as manifest in the other Christian scriptures are *traditions* that simply point to a clear awareness of the social and communal— that is to say, historical conditioning of God's symbolic self disclosure. We have already discussed the process of "traditioning" in our earlier considerations on the community of faith. Here we need only note that, as a process, "traditioning begins before the composition of the inspired books and continues without a break throughout the ages."[236] Because it embraces all three distinctions, tradition "is not static or simply preservative. It develops dynamically."[237] Dulles asserts that its

---

Dulles suggests that while this distinction was helpful for a time, the increase in secularity and the potential for a loss of "access" to the tradition, that is currently found in the late twentieth century, poses its own problems. Dulles contends that many of the faithful are, once again, hungering "for the richness and stability of a Catholic tradition to which they have almost lost access." He goes on: "While the recovery of stable tradition will not be easy, the signs of the times in the 1990s are in some respects more favorable to 'traditions' than those of the early 1960s." See, *The Craft of Theology,* 102.

[236]Dulles, *The Craft of Theology*, 96.

[237]Dulles, "Faith and Revelation," 121. Henceforth, the word "tradition" will be understood to be inclusive of all of its facets—unless one of its particular facets needs to be highlighted.

Another of Dulles' summary points on *Dei Verbum* can be highlighted at this point, namely, *"Development."* Dulles speaks of the "forward thrust" of tradition. He quotes again from *Dei Verbum*: "This tradition which comes from the apostles progresses

Continued on next page

dynamic nature makes tradition, when viewed from the standpoint of contemporary Catholicism, something that "cannot be adequately understood as a [mere] body of explicit teaching . . . In the words of Vatican Council II, tradition 'includes everything that contributes to the holiness of life and the increase of faith of the people of God' (*DV 8*)."[238]

Tradition, then, is in a state of perpetual "becoming" for the community of faith. Dulles invokes Maurice Blondel to argue that tradition has the ability "to transmit the lived reality of the past."[239] Moreover, "because revelation has an eschatological dimension, tradition too can be future-oriented. It *propels* the

---

in the Church under the assistance of the Holy Spirit . . . Thus, as the centuries advance, the Church constantly tends toward the fullness of divine truth, until the words of God reach their consummation in the Church" (DV 8). Dulles points out that "this progress does not occur by mere logical inference or by continuous, organic evolution, but through 'the practice and life of the believing and praying Church.'" See Dulles, *The Craft of Theology*, 95. See also Dulles, "Vatican II and the Recovery of Tradition," 86-90, specifically his considerations on the topic of "innovation." ["*Das II. Vatikanum und die Wiedergewinnung der Tradition, 556-560.*]

[238]Dulles, "Faith and Revelation," 121. Our *inclusio*. Further on, Dulles observes, again from *DV 8*, that "authentic tradition is to be found not only in formal statements but also in 'the practice and life of the believing and praying community.'"

[239]Dulles, "Vatican II and the Recovery of Tradition," 84. ["*Das II. Vatikanum und die Wiedergewinnung der Tradition,*" 554.] He refers here to the work of Maurice Blondel. See Blondel,

Continued on next page

church forward to the day of the Lord, when the church will fully come into its own."[240] "Tradition, then, is the bearer of what is tacitly known and thus of what cannot be expressed in clear, unambiguous statements . . . [Tradition] is the church's continuing capacity to interpret, to discern, to penetrate. Far from being a confining or retrograde force, it is a power of development and expansion."[241] As the community engages in the process of interpretation, discernment, and penetration of

---

History and Dogma (New York: Holt, Rinehart & Winston, 1964), especially 264-287.

[240]Dulles, "Faith and Revelation," 121. Our emphasis. See also Dulles, "Tradition and Creativity," 325: "Because Christ the Lord is 'the same yesterday, today, and tomorrow,' Christian tradition can rise to this challenge, ceaselessly bringing forth 'new things and old.'"

[241]Dulles, "Vatican II and the Recovery of Tradition," 84. ["*Das II. Vatikanum und die Wiedergewinnung der Tradition*," 554.] This is evidently influenced by the work of Polanyi. Two other summary points of Dulles on *DV* may be mentioned. The first point is: "*Tradition and traditions.*" Dulles points out that *DV* speaks of tradition in the singular. "Its concern is with tradition as an organ of apprehension and transmission rather than as a set of doctrines or precepts. Tradition is the mode in which the Church perpetuates its faith and its very existence (DV 8)." The second point: "*The means of 'traditioning.'* Dulles notes that *DV* insists on "the nonverbal elements in tradition: Christ communicates the gospel not by his words alone but also by his dealings with others and his behavior (DV 7). The apostles transmit the gospel not only by preaching [inclusive of the preaching, life and worship of the contemporary church] but also by example and ordinances (*institutiones*)." See Dulles, *The Craft of Theology,* 94-95.

revelatory symbols, the dialogue calls all its members to deeper insight and faith. It is clear that this dialogue, the intelligent discussion and exploration of the symbolic mediation of the self-communication of God, can take place only when all members of the community, are speaking out of the same tradition and experience. Consequently, the Second Vatican Council emphasized that "tradition arises through a real, living self-communication of God in grace and revelation, that it is rooted in the life of the community of faith, and that it adapts itself and develops in changing historical situations."[242]

A few remaining comments regarding the work of the Council need to be made. Dulles suggests that the Council's thought on tradition "resonates" with "Blondel's theory." Blondel's theory is one that Dulles, himself, seems to entertain. It involves, most notably, the understanding that tradition, restated in the words of Dulles,

> promotes the human and religious values that traditionalism tends to impede: personal judgment, direct experience, adaptation, responsible decision, and innovation. Authentic innovations, since they arise out of an experience of the very reality carried by the tradition, do not

---

[242]Dulles, "Vatican II and the Recovery of Tradition," 77. ["*Das II. Vatikanum und die Wiedergewinnung der Tradition,*" 547.]

erode the tradition but rather reinforce and revitalize it.[243]

In other words, tradition can only find place within a stance of faith and in a community of faith. Dulles writes, as follows, of the three features of this theory:

> In the first place, tradition is seen not as an end or an object in itself, but as a *means* whereby the church and its members can *enter* into a living relationship with God . . . Second, tradition is not seen primarily as a matter of word or propositional truth, but rather as something *communicated* through *action, example, and worship* . . . Finally, tradition is seen as *progressive and dynamic* rather than simply conservative and static.[244]

---

[243] Dulles, "Vatican II and the Recovery of Tradition," 90. ["*Das II. Vatikanum und die Wiedergewinnung der Tradition,*" 560.]

[244] Dulles, "Vatican II and the Recovery of Tradition," 90-91. ["*Das II. Vatikanum und die Wiedergewinnung der Tradition,*" 561.] Our emphasis. Dulles closes this section by suggesting that "it is therefore a matter of great urgency for Catholics to appreciate how the Constitution of Divine Revelation found ways of safeguarding the permanence and universality of God's gift in Christ while at the same time allowing for great fluidity in the formulations, customs, and practices by which that gift is communicated." See, "Vatican II and the Recovery of Tradition," 92. ["*Das II. Vatikanum und die Wiedergewinnung der Tradition,*" 562.] See also Dulles, *The Craft of Theology,* 92-93.

While Dulles may suggest that these three features "resonate" with Blondel, it is also quite apparent that they "resonate" with Dulles' ecclesial-transformative approach. Dulles' central themes—indwelling, participation, symbolic communication, transformation, and the *sensus fidelium*—are all suggested in the views of the Council. The ecclesial-transformative approach to revelation highlights, with profound intensity, the life-giving and life-sustaining tradition of the community of faith. As a means of indwelling and participation, tradition is communicated symbolically in action, example, and worship. Tradition calls forth responsibility, one that is, of course, nurtured and nourished by the very presence of God. In the *life* of the community itself, "the tradition is validated to the extent that it enables those who dwell in it to go beyond it and, so to speak, break out."[245] In short, the tradition is "progressive and dynamic." The tradition is ecclesial-transformative in nature.

---

[245]Dulles, "Vatican II and the Recovery of Tradition," 88. ["*Das Vatikanum und die Wiedergewinnung der Tradition,*" 558-559.] Dulles cites the dialectic of dwelling in and breaking out as found in Polanyi, *Personal Knowledge,* 195-202.

This is, for Dulles, perceived to be one of the "evaluative tools" of tradition. It also possesses an evident element that is "transformative" in nature. For further considerations on "evaluation," see Dulles, "Vatican II and the Recovery of Tradition," 88-90. ["*Das Vatikanum und die Wiedergewinnung der Tradition,*" 558-560.] Dulles speaks of the issue of "innovation" inherent to "tradition" and, at the same time, acknowledges the need for "limits and boundaries" (and hence, the role of the magisterium). Innovation must be involved in the process of
Continued on next page

The Teaching Authority of the Church

At the beginning of this section, we noted that Scripture, tradition and the magisterium are "inseparable and mutually interdependent." For the most part, the teaching authority of the Church does not experience any significant "redefinition" in light of the ecclesial-transformative structure. Dulles simply declares that "the organ that authoritatively expresses the mind of the Church is known as the ecclesiastical magisterium. The ordinary bearers of this magisterium are the pope and the bishops."[246] What must be noted, however, is that in order for the interdependent relationship of Scripture, tradition, and the magisterium to be life-giving, animating the symbolically mediated self-disclosure of God, and thus to be transformative of the church, the magisterium needs to be identified and connected with, needs to be responsive and responsible to, the community of faith.

We have said that the Scriptures must be read in light of the tradition; it is the context that shapes them. Moreover, this reading must take place "under the vigilance of the magisterium." The magisterium and the tradition, in turn, find their grounding in the Scriptures. Within the ecclesial-transformative approach to revelation, the teaching authority of the church plays a

---

"revitalization" but only within the context of the faith and the parameters of the faith community.

[246]Dulles, *The Craft of Theology*, 106.

substantial role as the organic entity—that is to say, faithful members of and full participants in a community of faith—that becomes responsible for the passing on of the faith. They are the "masters" who assist in the process of "apprenticeship." The process of traditioning embraces the understanding that "the message of Christ has to be proclaimed in new situations and interpreted for new audiences who have their own perspectives and their own questions. The ecclesiastical leadership must decide whether new hypotheses and formulations are acceptable in light of Christian faith."[247]

We have suggested that the coming to faith and the awareness and insight into the symbolic communication of God does not happen in isolation. It only happens within a living, dynamic, integrated community of faith. This is the point of departure for the teaching authority; it is the milieu within which such authorities must function—that is to say, if it is to be of

---

[247]Dulles, *The Craft of Theology,* 106. We submit yet another summary point of Dulles on *Dei Verbum: "Tradition and magisterium."* Dulles writes that "tradition, according to *Dei Verbum,* has been committed not to the magisterium alone but to the people of God as a whole (DV 10). All believers are responsible to hold fast to the faith and bear witness to it (*ibid.*)." Dulles adds, however, that "the magisterium is the sole authentic interpreter of the word of God, whether in written or nonwritten form." See, *The Craft of Theology,* 97. Dulles notes in a footnote (p. 206, n. 17) that "the term 'authentic' is a technical term that conveys the idea of authority exercised in the name of Christ." Cf. *DV* 10 and its corresponding footnotes.

service to the community and the revealed truth of God. There are, however, conflicting perceptions as to the breadth and scope of the magisterium. Some have suggested that the role and responsibility of the theologian, in the community of faith, is also an intimate part of the "teaching authority." Such a consideration would take us far beyond the scope of this work. We should note, however, that Dulles suggests that each group, the magisterium and the theologians, has specific tasks that are, in themselves, integral to the life of the church.

> The official teachers and the theologians use different methods and have different goals . . . Both theology and the ecclesiastical magisterium must operate in the context of the whole Church as the primary recipient and bearer of divine revelation.[248]

To be sure, the scholarship of theologians offers assistance in the magisterial role of interpreting the faith. Thus the magisterium and the theologians must be integrally connected, each being at the service of the other. At the same time, both must recognize that the ultimate point of termination of their work and ministry is the "whole Church," which is the "primary recipient and bearer of divine revelation."

According to Dulles, this is true as well for the interpretation of doctrinal statements. "The role of theology in

---

[248]Dulles, *The Craft of Theology*, 197.

reception and interpretation of doctrinal declarations [when the magisterium has spoken] is emphasized in the recent statement of the International Theological Commission on the hermeneutics of dogma. Dogmatic proclamation, according to this document, takes concrete form 'as a real, symbolic expression of the content of faith,' and 'contains and makes present what it designates.'"[249] Dulles goes on to say that "all doctrinal formulations, moreover, point beyond themselves to the mystery of God's own truth, which abides in the Church as a living subject. In a certain sense, therefore, even dogmatic declarations cannot be final."[250] Consequently, when the doctrinal formulations point beyond themselves and are not perceived as "final," the inherent truth of the statement—symbolically mediated and historically and culturally conditioned—becomes transformative for the Church, offering new penetrations into the truth of God's symbolic self-disclosure.

---

[249]Dulles, *The Craft of Theology,* 108. The internal quotes are taken from the International Theological Commission's document, "On the Interpretation of Dogmas," *Origins 20* (1990), 1-16. See especially, 12.

[250]Dulles, *The Craft of Theology,* 108.

Ten Theses Paradigmatic of the Ecclesial-Transformative Approach

Tradition is, indeed, a prominent feature in the ecclesial-transformative approach to revelation and theology. Its importance lies in tradition being the grounding and the source for all the other facets of the enterprise. Dulles offers ten theses that he believes "would probably receive broad, if not almost universal, support from Catholic theologians today."[251] It is quite possible that they also are paradigmatic of the features essential to Dulles' own symbolic theology and ecclesial-transformative approach.[252] These theses provide a closing summary for this section.

In the first thesis, Dulles suggests that "tradition involves a *communal 'sense of the faith'*" that is "aroused and continually sustained by the Holy Spirit." His second thesis is characterized by an understanding of that which offers "access to the tradition"—namely, life in the community of faith. As Dulles maintains throughout the development of his theory, the active life of the individual of faith, within the community of faith—that is to say, indwelling, participation, ritual, worship, moral action—is the gateway to insight.

---

[251]Dulles, *The Craft of Theology,* 103. See also Dulles, "Tradition and Creativity," 312-327.

[252]Dulles, *The Craft of Theology,* 103-104. See Dulles, "Tradition and Creativity," 319.

Dulles' third thesis bespeaks both the implicit and normative dimensions of the tradition. "Although tradition necessarily includes a tacit component, it has to some degree found normative expression in the writing of the fathers, in liturgical texts, and in other ecclesially certified 'monuments of tradition.'"[253] His fourth thesis is linked to the third. Tradition offers an "element of continuity" for the development of the doctrine of the faith and the on-going, perpetual life-creating force of the community.

Dulles maintains, in his fifth thesis, that tradition is "divine," "apostolic," and "living." It is aroused by a God who is actively, creatively, and dynamically working in the midst of humanity. Through the relationship that God shares with humanity, the tradition becomes a sustained, living entity, with its origins in the apostolic experience of Jesus Christ and extending into the present. As a living entity, rooted in the biblical expression of the faith of the community, it is held to be, in Dulles' sixth thesis, of "equal dignity" with Scripture.

---

[253]Dulles, *The Craft of Theology,* 103. These elements all help "sharpen" the sense of the faith of the community. See also Dulles, "Tradition and Creativity," 319: "The person of faith, especially the saint, grasps the profound meaning of past expressions of the faith by dwelling in a community of faith and acquiring a certain connaturality with the things of God . . . Tradition therefore expresses primarily by life and action and only secondarily by explicit statements." This statement captures the essential characteristics of the first four theses articulated by Dulles.

The tradition has been identified as a "resource for recognizing the canonical Scriptures" and is continually used as a "resource" for interpreting them. Dulles' seventh thesis explicitly addresses the interrelationship between Scripture and tradition. The eighth thesis states that "divine tradition gives rise to a variety of human traditions that mediate it to particular groups at particular times and places."[254] These human "traditions" are steadfast in their ability to offer a symbolic expression of the divine self-disclosure so that new insights and awarenesses may continually draw the faithful into a yet deeper relationship to God.

The ninth thesis addresses, in some sense, the role of the magisterium. For Dulles' enterprise, "symbols are not infinitely malleable," and he suggests that "human traditions, while needed to make divine tradition concrete and tangible, must constantly be scrutinized for their soundness and relevance."[255] Finally, in his tenth thesis, Dulles maintains that "the ecclesiastical magisterium, making use of Scripture and tradition, is the authoritative judge of the conformity of particular doctrines and practices, including human traditions, with the word of God."[256]

---

[254]Dulles, *The Craft of Theology,* 104. See also Dulles, "Tradition and Creativity," 324: "In a certain sense tradition may be regarded as the Christian mystery transmitting itself."

[255]Dulles, *The Craft of Theology,* 104.

[256]Dulles, *The Craft of Theology,* 104.

In the course of this extensive exploration of the ecclesial-transformative approach, and Dulles' understanding of the symbolic mediation of the divine self-disclosure, certain problems have surfaced. There are, as well, a multitude of benefits which this approach has to offer to the Church of today and of the future. What remains is to reflect briefly on these benefits and difficulties.

Evaluation and Critique of Dulles' Thought

Dulles is, truly, a synthetic and systematic theologian. His work exemplifies, time and time again, his ability to pull together incredible amounts of theological material and synthesize it in ways that capture the essence of particular theological considerations. His symbolic enterprise is one such example. The ecclesial-transformative approach to revelation, perceived as the symbolically mediated self-communication of God, is a characteristically Dullesian approach to a major theological notion. One problem that seems to surface, however, is the need for more detailed examination of certain issues. The implications of certain themes or ideas are not always addressed.

Some Concerns

One of the first significant concerns that arises in the symbolic epistemology and ecclesial-transformative approach of

Avery Dulles stems from what he considers a valuable consequence of this schema—namely, the potential for interfaith dialogue. Dulles suggests that all reality is symbolic, that human beings are, by nature, symbolic, and that the self-disclosure of the divine is symbolically mediated. He also asserts a plasticity of symbol that gives the symbol its power to speak to people in varying sociocultural situations. He believes that this plasticity allows for the possibility of dialogue between faith traditions. Thus he argues that "there can be a measure of equivalence or complementarity among diverse symbol systems."[257] At the same time, however, Dulles characterizes all revelation as symbolically mediated and, hence, as possessed of a "plenitude of meaning." Moreover, the revelation, from a Christian perspective, is concentrated in Christ Jesus. Tradition and the considerations of the sense of the faithful—indwelling, the community, and participation in its life of faith—constitute the interpretive framework for the symbolic mediation of the divine.

This is Dulles' *Sitz im Leben,* the framework within which Dulles executes theology, and it would be incongruous to think it possible for him to speak outside this context. Does this not, however, limit one's perceptual possibilities and potential insights into revelation? What about *other* meanings of the same experience of the divine? Is Dulles suggesting, on the one hand, that interfaith dialogue is possible by virtue of revelation's

---

[257]Dulles, *Models of Revelation*, 153. Cf. Dulles, "The
Continued on next page

symbolic character, and, on the other hand, that there can only be **one** singular meaning of an experience of revelation?[258]

Our interpretive framework—our social, cultural, historical environment—is the key element in the hermeneutics of experience. It fashions, influences, and contextualizes our very experience. Consequently, another question surfaces. Is the same experience, i.e., self-disclosure of the divine, in and from two differing interpretive frameworks, truly "the same?" From Dulles' point of reference, the Christian tradition and the *sensus fidelium* are the interpretive framework[259] that directs one towards and shapes the meaning of the self-communication of God. Does this not also incapacitate us in some sense? Does this interpretive framework really allow the benefits of a symbolic epistemology to come to the fore in interfaith dialogue? Does it not prevent us from being open to other meanings of other experiences from other interpretive frameworks? Dulles asserts the potential benefits of his enterprise. Nonetheless, it would be interesting to see how this enterprise fares in the actual practice and dialogue.

Symbolic Structure of Revelation, 57.

[258]See Dulles, "The Symbolic Structure of Revelation," 58. See also Dulles, *Models of Revelation,* 143, 151. See also Cook, "Revelation as Metaphoric Process," 401-411.

[259]See Dulles, *The Craft of Theology,* 78: "It is widely recognized today that we do not have some pure experience prior to thought and word, but that our experience is largely molded by
Continued on next page

Another concern, and, at the same time an apparent weakness, in Dulles' development of symbolic mediation and the ecclesial-transformative approach, involves his understanding of indwelling. We have covered, quite extensively, the recognition that indwelling has two aspects—namely, dwelling in the revelatory symbols **and** dwelling in the community of faith. Each of these carries a weakness that does not seem to be addressed by Dulles. In the first instance, Dulles suggests that to come to awareness and insight, to discover the truth embedded in the symbolic self-disclosure of God, one must dwell in the symbols within the experience of the community of faith. The question that Dulles does not seem to address is: Who does, ultimately, dwell in the symbols "well enough?" And furthermore, in the second instance, who is ultimately "qualified" or competent to interpret the revelatory symbols? It would seem that there is an underlying presupposition that "indwelling" can, (and must) in some sense, be qualitatively and quantitatively measured.[260] This issue, however, seems to be lost in his general considerations of and expectations of faithful people in a community of faith. This could be a potential problem when considering the socialization

---

the presuppositions and interpretative categories with which it is bound up."

[260]Polanyi suggests that "the more complex and profound a particular subject matter is, the higher degree of depth of indwelling required for understanding it." See Polanyi, *The Tacit Dimension,* 16, 18.

of the individual—or for that matter, the formation of the community itself.[261]

Another question arises with the topic of "competency." This involves the potential of the community to stray from the tradition. Contemporary culture and society offer a plethora of "trendy theological possibilities" and "ideological distractions." These have the ability to entice the community, no less than the individual, away from the revelatory truth of the symbols that are a part of the tradition. These symbols are, as Dulles has maintained, the vehicle that draws people into deeper insight and awareness of the transcendent reality of God. Dulles does not seem to take into account the idea of a "tainted" tradition. What keeps the community from "straying" in the first place? These questions are absent from Dulles' considerations.

Dulles suggests, in his appropriation of the work of John Henry Newman, specifically the *sensus fidelium,* that the dialogue that takes place in the interpretation of symbol, experiences of faith, is the medium that generates growth and ecclesial transformation. The dialogue is a consequent of the process of indwelling. This dialogue assists the individual towards a deeper sense of the faith. In turn, this deeper sense

---

[261]See Dulles, *The Craft of Theology,* 103: "Without a more effective socialization into the Church, the faithful may no longer be in a position to accept or to interpret correctly the Scriptures, the normative symbols, and the statements of faith that have come down from the past."

leads to "an ability to see the deficiencies in the ways that Christians have previously expressed their faith," and allows them to be "more creative . . . in adapting Christian doctrine and symbolism to new and unprecedented situations."[262] The problem remains that, although dialogue is spoken of in terms of the members of the community, there seems to be, on the one hand an apparently simplistic presumption of the supposed goodwill of all the participants in the discussion, and, on the other, a lack of consideration of the potential hidden agendas and self-interests of the participants.

Furthermore, in Dulles' discussion of the participants of the dialogue, seemingly understood as all members of the community—the laity, theologians, and Church leaders, i.e., magisterium—he also seems to suggest that only the magisterium are proficient in the process of interpretation and that the members must submit to the magisterium. There is an inherent contradiction here, which may be, in some sense, a problem that is a corollary to the one noted above. Indwelling is one of the more salient features of Dulles' work. It is a notion that is very "catholic," but not necessarily "Roman," in nature. Dulles seems to suggest that the one who dwells in the revelatory symbol and in the community of faith is obedient to the Church. This concern surfaces in his discussion of the magisterium as the official teachers and the official interpreters of the symbolic

---

[262]The reader is referred back to Chapter Three,
Continued on next page

communication of the divine.[263] It would seem that, when push comes to shove, Dulles simply lives within the tradition, within

---

"Indwelling," note 175 and *"Sensus Fidelium."*

[263]See Dulles, *The Communication of Faith and Its Content,* 16. See also Dulles, *The Craft of Theology,* 105-118; "Revelation and Discovery," 26; "Faith, Church, and God," 540-541.

See also Lindbeck, "Dulles on Method," 53-62. Lindbeck points out that while there are many of Dulles' views that make "eminently good sense," one area in particular, that of "the communication medium," does not. In essence, the difference between Lindbeck and Dulles is the "relative priority" between symbolic realism and the biblical narrative as the media for the self-communication of the divine. Lindbeck suggests (p. 53) that Dulles' aims would be better served if he "balanced his emphasis on 'real symbols' by a recognition of the criteriological primacy of 'realistic narrative.'" In other words (p. 60), Dulles' "Method of Models would be improved by adherence to the hermeneutical primacy of realistic narrative in scriptural interpretation." Lindbeck points out (p. 57) that the Dullesian use of "Rahnerian symbolic realism in explaining how God makes himself cognitively accessible in faith and knowledge to human beings" is flawed. He suggests, in the same place, that the category of "realistic narrative can better incorporate the strengths of precritical Bible reading without excluding historical criticism, i.e., without lapsing into either countercriticism or paracriticism." For further clarification the reader is refered to Footnotes 1 and 2, located on page 57 of this article.

Lindbeck also suggests (p. 58) that "there are occasions . . . when the *lex credendi* guides the *lex orandi,* and then the primacy in theological interpretation of symbol or narrative may make a difference." Moreover, the "objection of narrativists . . . to the primacy of real symbol . . . is that the logic of symbols, unlike that of realistic narratives, is transitive."

Dulles emphatically points out, in his rejoinder to George Lindbeck (p. 61-62) that the choice between symbolic realism and biblical realistic narrative "cannot be exclusive." He goes on to
Continued on next page

the system, and does not engage the Church in its own transformation—that is to say, does not challenge it.

Given the growing separation between the official teachers and the lived experience of the laity, who are more educated, or at least more informed than ever before in matters of theology and faith, the symbolic epistemology of the ecclesial-transformative approach to revelation and theology has incredible potential for the transformation of the Church, itself, as an organic, living entity. The stage is set with the work Dulles has accomplished.[264] Yet, it appears as if there might be some critical, inherent, tensions that would prevent the work from

---

assert that "the principal Christian symbols (such as the cross, the empty tomb) derive their meaning and power from the narrative context in which they were forged." Dulles stresses that "'symbolic communication,' therefore, should not be reduced to particular symbols seen in isolation." "Revelation regularly takes place through 'symbolic communication;' sometimes, very importantly, through realistic biblical narrative."

Dulles also makes reference (p. 62) to Lindbeck's suggestion that creeds and dogmas are an "ecclesial and doctrinal detour" in an attempt to "preserve the true content of biblical faith from being obscured by a symbolic hermeneutical process." Dulles responds to this objection by pointing out that he (Dulles) has "sought to show, on the contrary, that the church's dogma is a fruit of that very process. It gathers up the explicit and latent meanings of the biblical texts and symbols, and protects them from distortions."

[264]See Dulles, *The Craft of Theology,* wherein the first two chapters are, for all intents and purposes, oriented to this topic.

continuing, and thus prevent the possibilities for transformation being realized.

It has been suggested, in earlier of this chapter, regarding the traditioning of the community and the teaching of the skills necessary for the discovery of God and the indwelling of the symbols through the community of faith, that this is a process for neophytes. We have asserted, throughout, that it is, also, a process for the "life members," a continuing formation of growth in one's life of faith and of the community. Dulles neglects this aspect in his writings. He continually focuses solely on converts to the faith. This is a drawback. The potential of the dynamics of his enterprise to effect powerful transformation, a key element in his own work, on the life of all the members of the Church, is immense.[265]

It could be said that the weakness of Dulles' system is not in the system itself. The weakness, or the drawback *per se,* lies in the fact that many of its implications are left unconsidered. There is, however, one other problem. We have pointed out that "dogmatic proclamation, according to the document from the International Theological Commission, takes concrete form 'as a real, symbolic expression of the content of faith,' and 'contains and makes present what it designates.'"[266] (Dulles raises this issue in his section on the magisterium and its

---

[265]See Dulles, *The Craft of Theology,* 53-68 and, specifically, his considerations on conversion.
[266]See Dulles, *The Craft of Theology,* 108.

role in the articulation of church teaching). At first glance, it appears that Dulles is hinting at a more cognitive-propositional approach (albeit symbolic) than an ecclesial-transformative one. He points out that "all doctrinal formulations, moreover, point beyond themselves to the mystery of God's own truth, which abides in the Church as a living subject. In a certain sense, therefore, even dogmatic declarations cannot be final."[267] It could be argued that Dulles occasionally slips into a "cognitive-propositional" approach, one which perceives symbols as subordinate to propositional speech.

Some Benefits

Throughout this work, we have emphasized the positive and beneficial aspects of Dulles' symbolic enterprise. They are considerable. Two further benefits, implicitly suggested in the work, need to be stressed here. One concerns an issue that is currently in dire need of attention in the Church—namely, tolerance. The other concerns the relationship between the community of faith, the contemporary society, and the world at large.

Dulles' understanding of the human being as symbolic and, more specifically, symbolic communication itself is, in one sense, a plea for tolerance. Dulles maintains, throughout his

---

[267]Dulles, *The Craft of Theology*, 108.

enterprise, the richness of the symbol. He speaks, quite emphatically, on the ability of the symbol to provide a multitude of meaning that stems from its multifarious nature. Symbol and symbolism provide a climate broad enough, and strong enough, to tolerate all kinds of expression. Dulles suggests, of course, that, in the Christian framework, the revelatory symbol can only be balanced off, and interpreted, in light of the Risen Christ. Even so Dulles' framework is not as limiting as one might initially suspect.

The symbolic and ecclesial-transformative schema offers considerable freedom of exploration and discovery. If one is not initially threatened by an unfounded concern for the potential loss of the objective truth in these multivalent symbols, then it becomes evident that the multiplicity of possible interpretations will not affect the tradition (an attendant concern). The interpretive framework, consequently, has the ability to become a fuller, richer, and more densely nourishing environment for people of faith. Perceived in this manner as a "plea for tolerance," the ecclesial-transformative approach can call people to be open to consider other expressions of the saving realities of God's self-disclosure.

The final benefit of Dulles' enterprise simply addresses one of that enterprise's more fundamental elements from a different perspective. The very essence of his work is located in the experience of God and the community. This experience has, for Dulles, a uniquely ecclesial-transformative dimension. As such, Dulles' enterprise seems to demand a particular way of life. This demand involves a life that is ultimately oriented to God, and in service of each other, to the community—the church—contemporary society, and the world. In one sense, this way of life calls for a re-examination of our relationship to those around us—individuals, other religions, other nations—and to our earthly resources. In another sense it simply may be reduced to our responsibility to "our neighbor" that flows from the dynamic, transformative, salvific, revelation of God. With a fundamental grounding in the community of faith, the place where "God dwells," the possibilities for transformation of church and of the world take root.

Postscript

Early, in *Models of Revelation,* Dulles explores the issue of "the function of revelation in modern Christianity."[268] He suggests that Christian theologians from various backgrounds, all readily recognize the centrality of revelation. He quotes the Dutch Calvinist, Herman Bavinck, who asserted, early in the twentieth century, that,

> with the reality of revelation, therefore, Christianity stands or falls . . . As science never precedes life, but always follows it and flows

---

[268]Dulles, *Models of Revelation*, 3.

from it, so the science of the knowledge of God
rests on the reality of his revelation. If God does
not exist, or if he has not revealed himself, and
hence is unknowable, then all religion is an illusion
and all theology a phantasm.[269]

Dulles, himself, speaks no less emphatically when he identifies
revelation as a foundation for all theology. "Theology **cannot**
maintain its identity and vigor if it overlooks this foundational
category."[270]

But Dulles's understanding of revelation is distinctive.
Revelation, for him, is the symbolically mediated self-expression
and self-communication of God. Dulles holds, moreover, this
understanding of symbolic mediation to be determinative for all
contemporary theological thought. Dulles' closing paragraph of
Models of Revelation offers an appropriate end to our
exploration of his work.

How, then, is revelation related to theology? In
the symbolic or postcritical approach, revelation
is accepted, at least by tacit faith, from the
beginning. Insofar as it places explicit trust in the
Church, with its normative sources, symbols, and
traditions of interpretation, theology takes shape

---

[269]Dulles, *Models of Revelation,* 5. Dulles quotes H.
Bavinck, *The Philosophy of Revelation. The Stone Lectures for
1908-1909* (Grand Rapids: Eerdmans, 1953), 20 and 24.

[270]Dulles, *Models of Revelation,* ix. Our emphasis.

as a specific discipline with a distinct methodology. Revelation, rather than being presupposed as fully known from the start, is progressively elucidated as theology carries out its task. As the joint meaning of all the clues and symbols whereby God communicates himself, revelation is the source and center, the beginning and the end, of the theological enterprise.[271]

---

[271]Dulles, *Models of Revelation,* 283.

SELECTED BIBLIOGRAPHY

Primary Sources

Books by Avery Dulles

DULLES, Avery. *The Assurance of Things Hoped For: A Theology of Christian Faith*. New York: Oxford University Press, 1994.

_____. *The Catholicity of the Church*. Oxford: Clarendon Press, 1985.

_____. *A Church to Believe In: Discipleship and the Dynamics of Freedom*. New York: Crossroad, 1984.

_____. *Communication of Faith and Its Content*. Washington, D.C.: National Catholic Educational Association, 1985.

_____. *The Craft of Theology: From Symbol to System*. New York: Crossroad, 1992 [Expanded Edition, 1995].

_____. *Models of the Church*. Garden City, New York: Doubleday and Co., 1974.

_____. *Models of Revelation*. Maryknoll, New York: Orbis Books, 1992.

_____. *The Reshaping Catholicism: Current Challenges in the Theology of Church*. New York: Harper & Row, 1988.

_____. *The Resilient Church: The Necessity and Limits of Adaptation*. Dublin: Gill and Macmillan, Ltd., 1978.

_____. *Revelation and the Quest for Unity*. Cleveland: Corpus, 1968.

_____. *Revelation Theology: A History*. New York: Herder and Herder, 1969.

_____. *The Survival of Dogma: Faith, Authority, and Dogma in a Changing World*. New York: Crossroad, 1987.

Primary Sources

Articles by Avery Dulles

DULLES, Avery. "Authority and Reason in the Ascent of Faith." In *Spirit, Faith, and Church*, ed. Wolfhart Pannenberg, Avery Dulles, Carl E. Braaten, 32-50. Philadelphia: Westminster Press, 1970.

_____. "The Authority of Scripture: A Catholic Perspective." In *Scripture in the Jewish and Christian Traditions: Authority, Interpretation, Relevance*, ed. Frederick E. Greenspahn, 9-40. Nashville: Abingdon, 1982.

_____. *"Das II. Vatikanum und die Wiedergewinnung der Tradition."* In *Glaube im Prozess: Christsein nach dem II. Vatikanum - Für Karl Rahner*, ed. Elmar Klinger and Klaus Wittstadt, 546-562. Freiburg im Breisgau: Herder, 1984.

_____. "Faith and Revelation." In *Systematic Theology: Roman Catholic Perspectives, Volume 1*, ed. Francis Schüssler Fiorenza and John P. Galvin, 92-128. Minneapolis: Fortress Press, 1991.

_____. "Faith, Church, and God: Insights from Michael Polanyi." *Theological Studies 45* (1984), 537-550.

_____. "From Images to Truth: Newman on Revelation and Faith." *Theological Studies 51* (1990), 252-267.

_____. "The Meaning of Revelation." In *The Dynamic in Christian Thought,* ed. Joseph Papin, 52-80. Philadelphia: Villanova University Press, 1970.

_____. "Modern Credal Affirmations." In *Foundation Documents of the Faith,* ed. Cyril S. Rodd, 125-140. Edinburgh: T. & T. Clark Limited, 1987.

_____. "Official Church Teaching and Historical Relativity." In *Spirit, Faith, and Church,* ed. Wolfhart Pannenberg, Avery Dulles, Carl E. Braaten, 51-72. Philadelphia: Westminster Press, 1970.

_____. "Paths to Doctrinal Agreement: Ten Theses." *Theological Studies 47* (1986), 32-47.

_____. "The Problem of Revelation." In *Proceedings of the Catholic Theological Society of America 29* (1974), 77-106. [With responses from Myles M. Bourke, 107-116 and Gabriel Moran, F.S.C., 117-123].

_____. "Revelation." In *An American Catholic Catechism,* ed. George J. Dyer, 3-15. New York: Seabury Press, 1975.

_____. "Revelation." In *New Encyclopedia Britannica: Macropedia 15,* 783-786. Chicago: Encyclopædia Britannica, Inc., 1974.

_____. "Revelation and Discovery." In *Theology and Discovery: Essays in Honor of Karl Rahner, S.J.,* ed. William J. Kelly, 1-29. Milwaukee: Marquette University Press, 1980. [With responses from Joseph T. Lienhard, S.J., 30-33 and Andrew Tallon, 34-37].

_____. "Symbol in Revelation." In *The New Catholic Encyclopedia,* ed. The Catholic University of America, 861-863. New York: McGraw-Hill Co, 1967.

_____. "The Symbolic Structure of Revelation." *Theological Studies 41* (1980), 51-73.

_____. "Tradition and Creativity: A Theological Approach." In *The Quadrilog: Tradition and the Future of Ecumenism, Essays in Honor of George H. Tavard,* ed. Kenneth Hagan, 317-327. Collegeville: The Liturgical Press, A Michael Glazier Book, 1994.

_____. "Vatican II and Communications." In *Vatican II: Assessment and Perspectives, Twenty-Five Years After (1962-1987).* 3 Volumes, ed. René Latourelle, 528-547. Mahwah: Paulist Press, 1988.

Related Sources

Books

ABBOTT, Walter M., ed. *The Documents of Vatican II.* Piscataway, New Jersey: America Press/New Century Publishers, Inc., 1966.

AUGUSTINE. *Confessions.* Translated by Rex Warner. New York: Mentor- Omega Books, 1963.

BERNARD, Charles A. *Théologie symbolique.* Paris: Téqui, 1978.

BLONDEL, Maurice. *History and Dogma.* New York: Holt, Rinehart and Winston, 1964.

DAVIS, Charles. *Religion and the Making of Society: Essays in Social Theology.* Cambridge: Cambridge University Press, 1994.

DE JONG, P. *Die Eucharistie als symbolwirklichkeit.* Regensburg, 1969.

DE LUBAC, Henri. *La révélation divine,* Paris: Cerf, 1983.

FRANSEN, Piet. *The New Life of Grace.* Translated by George DuPont, S.J. London: Goeffrey Chapman, 1969.

GESCHÉ, Adolphe. *Dieu pour penser, II: L'homme.* Paris: Cerf, 1993.

GILKEY, Langdon. *Naming the Whirlwind.* Indianapolis: Bobbs-Merrill, 1969.

HAMMAN, A. G. *L'homme, Image de Dieu: Essai d'une anthropologie chrétienne dans l'Eglise des cinq premiers siècles,* Relais-Études 2. Paris: Desclée, 1987.

HÄRING, Bernhard. *Free and Faithful in Christ,* 2 Volumes. New York: Seabury/Crossroad, 1979.

HICK, John. *Faith and Knowledge.* Ithaca: Cornell University Press, 1957.

LATOURELLE, René. *Théologie de la révélation.* [Theology of Revelation]. Bruges: Desclée de Brouwer, 1963. [Staten Island: Alba House, 1966].

LINDBECK, George. *The Nature of Doctrine: Religion and Theology in a Postliberal Age.* Philadelphia: Westminster, 1984.

MARSHALL, Bruce D., ed. *Theology and Dialogue: Essays in Conversation with George Lindbeck.* Notre Dame: University of Notre Dame Press, 1990.

MORAN, Gabriel. *The Present Revelation: In Quest of Religious Foundations.* New York: Herder and Herder, 1972.

NEWMAN, John Henry. *An Essay in Aid of a Grammar of Assent.* Garden City: Doubleday Image Book, 1955.

_____. *Fifteen Sermons Preached before the University of Oxford*. London: Longmans, Green and Co., 1892.

_____. *On Consulting the Faithful in Matters of Doctrine*. Edited by John Coulson. London: Collins Liturgical Publications, 1961.

O'COLLINS, Gerald. *Retrieving Fundamental Theology: The Three Styles of Contemporary Theology*. Mahwah: Paulist Press, 1993.

O'DONOVAN, Leo and HOWLAND Sanks, ed. *Faithful Witness: Foundations of Theology for Today's Church*. New York: Crossroad, 1989.

POLANYI, Michael and H. PROSCH. *Meaning*. Chicago: University of Chicago Press, 1975.

POLANYI, Michael. *Personal Knowledge: Towards a Post-Critical Philosophy*. New York: Harper and Row, Harper Torchbooks, 1964

_____. *The Tacit Dimension*. Garden City: Doubleday/Anchor Books, 1967.

RAHNER, Karl. *Foundations of Christian Faith*. New York: Crossroad, 1989.

RICŒUR, Paul. *Symbolism of Evil*. Boston: Beacon, 1969.

_____. Emmanuel Levinas, Edgar Haulotte, Etienne Cornélis, Claude Geffré. *La révélation*. Bruxelles: Facultés universitaires Saint-Louis, 1984.

SCHILLEBEECKX, Edward and Bas van Iersel, ed. *Revelation and Experience, Concilium 113*. New York: Crossroad/Seabury Press, 1979.

SEGUNDO, Juan Luis. *The Liberation of Dogma: Faith, Revelation, and Dogmatic Teaching Authority*. Maryknoll, New York: Orbis Books, 1992.

SHORTER, Aylward. *Revelation and its Interpretation*. London: Geoffrey Chapman, 1983.

SOUKOP, Paul A. *Communication and Theology*. London: World Association for Christian Communication, 1983.

TILLICH, Paul. *Systematic Theology*. Chicago: University of Chicago Press, 1951.

URBAN, Wilbur M. *Language and Reality*. London: Allen & Unwin, 1939.

VATICAN I DOCUMENTS. *Dei Filius. Enchiridion symbolorum, definitionum et declarationum de rebus fidei et morum,* ed. H. Denzinger; 32nd ed., revised by A. Schönmetzer. Freiburg im Breisgau: Herder, 1963.

VORGRIMLER, Herbert, ed. *Commentary on the Documents of Vatican II, Volume III.* New York: Herder and Herder, 1969.

WHEELWRIGHT, P. H. *Metaphor and Reality*. Bloomington: Indiana University Press, 1962.

Related Sources

Articles

BRETON, Stanislas. *"Révélation, médiation, manifestation."* In *Philosophie - Manifestation et Révélation,* ed. *Faculté de Philosophie, Institut Catholique de Paris,* 41-61. Paris: *Éditions Beauchesne,* 1976.

COOK, Michael L. "Revelation As Metaphoric Process." *Theological Studies 47* (1986), 388-411.

CONGREGATION FOR THE DOCTRINE OF THE FAITH. "Instruction on the Ecclesial Vocation of the Theologian." *Origins 20* (1990), 117-126.

CRÜSEMANN, Frank. "'You Know the Heart of a Stranger' (Exodus 23:9). A Recollection of the Torah in the Face of New Nationalism and Xenophobia." *Concilium 1993/4, Migrants and Refugees.* New York: Crossroad/Seabury Press, 1993. 95-109.

DE SCHRIJVER, George. "Hermeneutics and Tradition." In *Authority in the Church, Annua Nuntia Louvaniensia XXVI,* ed. Piet Fransen, 32-47. Leuven: Leuven University Press, 1983.

HUGHSON, Thomas. "Dulles and Aquinas on Revelation." *The Thomist* 52 (1988), 445-471.

INTERNATIONAL THEOLOGICAL COMMISSION. "Interpretation of Dogmas." *Origins 20* (1990), 1-16.

KELLY, Justin, J. "Knowing by Heart: The Symbolic Structure of Revelation and Faith." In *Faithful Witness: Foundations of Theology for Today's Church,* eds. Leo J. O'Donovan and T. Howland Sanks, 63-84. New York: Crossroad, 1989.

LINDBECK, George A. "Dulles on Method." *Pro Ecclesia* 1 (1994), 53-60. [With a rejoinder by Avery Dulles, S.J., 61-62].

LIBERATORE, Albert. "Symbols in Rahner: A Note on Translation." *Louvain Studies* 18 (1993), 145-158.

MATTES, Marc C. Review of *The Craft of Theology: From Symbol to System,* by Avery Dullas, S.J., In *Dialog,* Volume 34, Number 2 (Spring, 1995), 144-146.

MERRIGAN, Terrence. "The Craft of Theology." *Louvain Studies* 18 (1993), 243-257.

_____. "Models in the Theology of Avery Dulles: A Critical Analysis." *Bijdragen, tijdschrift voor filosofie en theologie* 54 (1993), 141-161.

MITCHELL, Nathan. "Symbols are Actions, Not Objects." *Living Worship 13/2* (1977), 1-4.

POLANYI, Michael. "Faith and Reason." *The Journal of Religion* 41 (1961), 237-247.

RAHNER, Karl. "*Über den Begriff des Geheimnisses in der katholischen Theologie.*" *Schriften zur Theologie, Band IV.* 51-99. ["The Concept of Mystery in Catholic Theology." *Theological Investigations IV: More Recent Writings.* Translated by Kevin Smyth. New York: Crossroad, 1966. 36-73.]

_____. "Man (Anthropology). III. Theological." *Encyclopedia of Theology.* New York: Seabury/Crossroad, 1975. 887-893.

_____. "Revelation." In *Revelation and Tradition,* ed. Karl Rahner and Joseph Ratzinger. Translated by W. J. O'Hara. New York: Herder and Herder, 1966.

_____. "*Theologie und Anthropologie.*" *Schriften zur Theologie, Band VII.* 43-65. ["Theology and Anthropology." *Theological Investigations IX: Writings of 1965-1967 I.* Translated by Graham Harrison. London: Darton, Longman & Todd, 1972. 28-45.]

_____. "Theology. I. Nature." *Encyclopedia of Theology.* New York: Seabury/Crossroad, 1975. 1686-1695.

_____. "*Zur Theologie der Menschwerdung.*" *Schriften zur Theologie, Band IV: Neuere Schriften. 137-155.* ["On the Theology of the Incarnation." *Theological Investigations*

IV: More Recent Writings. Translated by Kevin Smyth. New York: Crossroad, 1966. 105-120.]

_____."Zur Theologie des Symbols." *Schriften zur Theologie, Band IV: Neuere Schriften. 275-311.* ["The Theology of the Symbol." *Theological Investigations IV: More Recent Writings*. Translated by Kevin Smyth. New York: Crossroad, 1966. 221-252.]

TILLICH, Paul. "*Die Idee der Offenbarung.*" In *Zeitschrift für Theologie und Kirche: Der neuen Folge 8*. Tübingen: Mohr, 1929. 403-412.

UNITED STATES BISHOPS COMMITTEE. "Doctrinal Responsibilities: Approaches to Promoting Cooperation and Resolving Misunderstandings between Bishops and Theologians." *Origins 19* (1989), 97-110.

VERGOTE, Antoine. "The Chiasm of Subjective and Objective Functions in the Symbol." In *Explorations de l'Espace théologique: Études de théologie et de philosophie de la religion. Bibliotheca Ephemeridum Theologicarum Lovaniensium, XC* Leuven: Leuven University Press, 1990. 471-493.

Reference/Background Sources

Books

HART, Ray L. *Unfinished Man and the Imagination: Toward an Ontology and a Rhetoric of Revelation*. New York: Herder and Herder, 1968.

LAMB, Matthew. *Solidarity with Victims: Toward a Theology of Social Transformation*. New York: Crossroad, 1982.

LASH, Nicholas. *Easter in Ordinary: Reflections on Human Experience and the Knowledge of God.* University of Virginia: SCM Press, 1988.

MERRIGAN, Terrence. *Clear Heads and Holy Hearts: The Religious and Theological Ideal of John Henry Newman.* Louvain Theological and Pastoral Monographs 7. Louvain: Peeters Press, W. B. Eerdmans, 1991.

NEWMAN, John Henry. *Newman The Theologian: A Reader,* ed. Ian Ker. Notre Dame: University of Notre Dame Press, 1990.

O'COLLINS, Gerald. *Fundamental Theology.* New York: Paulist Press, 1981.

PEPPER, Stephen. *World Hypotheses: A Study in Evidence.* Berkeley: University of California Press, 1942.

PERRIN, Norman. *Jesus and the Language of the Kingdom.* Philadelphia: Fortress, 1976.

SCHMAUS, Michael. *Dogma 1: God in Revelation.* Kansas City and London: Sheed and Ward, 1978.

Reference/Background Sources

Articles

COLLINS, Raymond F. "Inspiration." In *The New Jerome Biblical Commentary,* ed. Raymond E. Brown, Joseph A. Fitzmyer, and Roland E. Murphy, 1023-1033. Englewood Cliffs, New Jersey: Prentice Hall, 1990.

GRISEZ, Germain. "The Relationship Between God and Sinful Humankind." In *The Way of the Lord Jesus, Volume I, Christian Moral Principles,* 477-505. Chicago: Franciscan Herald Press, 1983.

PACKER, James I. "Contemporary Views of Revelation." In *Revelation and the Bible: Contemporary Evangelical Thought,* ed. Carl F. H. Henry, 89-104. London: Tyndale Press, 1958.

Theses and Dissertations

McAREE, F. J. "Revelation, Faith, and Mystery: The Theology of Revelation in the Writings of Avery Dulles." PHD Dissertation, Gregorian University, 1983.

SANDERS, Andries Frans. "Michael Polanyi's Post-Critical Epistemology: A Reconstruction of Some Aspects of 'Tacit Knowing.'" PHD Dissertation, Rijksuniversiteit te Groningen, 1988. [Amsterdam: Rodopi, 1988].

SHECTERLE, Ross A. "Redemptive Suffering: A Critical Re-Evaluation of Human Suffering and Divine Providence." Master of Divinity Thesis, St. Francis Seminary and School of Pastoral Ministry, 1985.

INDEX

—A—

anthropology, vii, 9-10, 13, 40-46, 49, 64-65, 68, 70, 82
Aquinas, 29, 136
attending from, 58, 60, 63, 89
attending to, 58, 63, 129
Augustine, 38, 108, 131

—B—

Barbour, Ian G., 48
Bavinck, Herman, 204-205
Blondel, Maurice, 181, 183, 185

—C—

Christ, 3, 10-11, 16, 18, 21, 32-34, 36, 43, 45, 64, 89, 91-92, 103, 105, 109-110, 116, 140, 143, 145-148, 150, 152, 156, 159, 162, 168, 182, 184, 187, 191, 194, 203
church, i-ii, vi, viii, xv, 2-3, 10, 15, 25-27, 29-32, 34, 36, 42, 63, 71, 79, 80-81, 90-92, 104-106, 108-109, 113-114, 123, 126, 128, 130-131, 136, 139, 141, 144, 147, 150-152, 155-156, 159-160, 162, 164, 166-167, 169, 172-173, 177, 179, 181-182, 184, 186, 188-189, 193, 197-202, 204-205

community, iv-vi, ix, 5, 9, 14-15, 24-25, 28-30, 38, 49, 71, 75-76, 78, 84, 88-89, 91-93, 96, 103-104, 106-107, 112, 114, 116-117, 120-121, 125-127, 130-132, 134, 136-140, 142, 144-145, 152-153, 155-166, 169-173, 175-176, 179-181, 184-191, 194, 196-198, 201-203
community of faith, iv, ix, 10, 16, 24-25, 28-30, 38, 88-89, 92, 103-104, 106-107, 114, 116-117, 120-121, 127, 130, 132, 134, 136-137, 139, 140, 142, 144, 153, 155, 157-158, 160-162, 165, 170, 176, 179-181, 184-188, 190-191, 196, 198, 201-202, 204
conversion, viii, 59-60, 90, 93, 118-119, 131, 143, 157, 161, 162, 169-170, 201
Cook, Michael L., ii, 99, 146, 195
Crüsemann, Frank, 44

—D—

Davis, Charles, 69
De Schrijver, George, 79-80
Dei Filius(DF), xv, 94-95
Dei Verbum(DV), xv, 91, 120, 147-148, 150-152, 156, 173, 176-177, 181-182, 187
deity, 1
discovery, i, viii, 12-13, 38, 58, 60-61, 63, 73, 88, 90, 92, 97, 108, 119-120, 123, 141, 164, 171, 177, 201, 203

divine, v-vii, 2, 4, 8-9, 12, 14, 17,
21-22, 25, 27, 34-35, 40, 52,
54-55, 64-65, 69-70, 73, 77-78,
80, 83-87, 89, 95-97, 100-101,
103, 106-107, 110, 112, 114,
116-122, 124-125, 127-128,
130, 133, 135-136, 140-141,
144-146, 152, 155-157, 164,
170, 172, 174, 177-178, 181,
188, 191-192, 194-195, 199
doctrine, vii, viii, 3, 4, 7, 9, 11-12,
19, 20-23, 25, 31, 33-34, 36,
37, 72, 75, 79-81, 83, 114, 118,
123, 131, 135-136, 146, 154,
156, 168, 172-173, 191, 198
Dulles, Avery, ii, vi-ix, 2-11, 13-
14, 16-19, 21-40, 43, 46-69, 71-
78, 80-116, 118-132, 134-139,
141-144, 146-206

—E—

ecclesia, 155, 169
Eliade, M., 56
epistemology, 4, 58, 63, 85-86,
136, 193, 195, 200

—F—

faith, iii-vi, viii-ix, 5, 8, 10-11, 16,
22, 24-30, 32, 35-36, 38, 52,
74, 88-89, 91-92, 95, 103-104,
106-107, 109, 112-117, 119-
121, 127, 130-135, 137-143,
147-149, 153, 155-159, 161-
166, 168-171, 173-176, 179-
182, 184-191, 194, 196-205
Fransen, Piet, 14-15, 64, 79

—G—

Gaudium et Spes(GS), xv, 43, 147,
150
Gesché, Adolphe, 45

God, i, iv-vii, ix, 2-5, 7-10, 12-18,
21-22, 25, 29-35, 37-49, 54, 61,
65, 69, 72, 77, 80, 82, 84-101,
103-104, 106, 108-110, 112-
114, 116-120, 122-127, 130-
131, 133-134, 136-138, 140-
141, 143-153, 155-156, 158-
159, 161-162, 164-169, 171-
172, 175-181, 183-184, 186-
187, 189, 191-193, 195-197,
199, 201-203, 205-206
grace, 10, 14, 22, 34, 64, 65, 71,
86, 119, 122, 142, 145, 147,
183

—H—

Hamman, A. G., 45
Häring, Bernhard, 17-18
Heidegger, Martin, 72
Hughson, Thomas, 29, 136
human (human being), vii, 1-2, 4-5,
8-9, 12-16, 18, 26, 30, 32-33,
35, 37-38, 40-49, 52, 54, 56-57,
59-60, 65-70, 72-74, 77-80, 83-
84, 86, 89-90, 95, 97-103, 105,
110-111, 114-115, 118-120,
122-124, 130, 144-146, 149,
152, 158, 169, 176, 183, 192-
193, 199, 202

—I—

illative, 136
immanence, 37, 43
incarnation, 12, 43, 47
indwelling, viii, 25, 28-29, 58, 63,
72, 75, 94, 128, 130-132, 134,
136, 176, 185, 190, 194, 196-
197, 201

insight, ii, vi-vii, 12, 23, 37, 42-43, 57, 59, 87, 93, 97, 105, 108, 110, 119, 122, 124, 133, 136, 141, 165, 173, 183, 187, 190, 196-197

—J—

Jesus, 3, 18, 32-33, 36, 42-43, 45-47, 88-90, 92, 103, 108-110, 125, 144-145, 147-150, 156, 159, 162, 167-168, 191, 194

—K—

Kelly, Justin J., 2, 13, 53, 67, 74, 90, 92, 97-100, 108-113, 117, 132-133, 144, 148-149, 161-162, 167-168
knowledge, ii, vii, 4, 24-26, 28-30, 32-33, 52, 57-59, 62-64, 69, 72-75, 86, 88-90, 97, 99-100, 108, 112-113, 117, 119, 121, 123-125, 127-130, 132-136, 138, 140-142, 155, 158-159, 165, 168-169, 171, 199, 205

—L—

language, 4, 24, 26, 40, 42, 46, 48, 50- 51, 53-55, 61, 63, 68-71, 74, 76-81, 87, 90, 93, 95-97, 99, 101-103, 111-112, 115, 118, 121-122, 132-133, 138, 140-141, 144, 149, 174, 177
Lateran Council, 147
Latourelle, René, 31, 148
Levinas, Emmanuel, 62
Liberatore, Albert, 50-51, 150
Lindbeck, George A., vii-viii, 11, 19, 20-25, 27, 29, 75, 118, 123-124, 131, 135, 154-155, 178, 199, 200
logos(λογος), 8, 36, 77, 105

Lumen Gentium, xv, 105, 151

—M—

Macquarrie, John, 171
Magisterium, 172
Mattes, Marc C., 29, 81
Merrigan, Terrence, ii, 131, 135, 137, 139
Mitchell, Nathan, 57-58

—N—

new awareness, 31, 37-38, 91
Newman, John Henry, viii, 28, 80, 135-137, 139, 141-142, 168, 197

—P—

Perrin, Norman, 124-125
Polanyi, Michael, viii, 25, 28, 53, 58, 63, 71-72, 83, 85, 90, 98, 109, 128-129, 131, 136-137, 142, 157, 163, 165, 182, 185, 196
propositional, 20, 22, 30-32, 78, 80, 91, 123, 155, 174, 184, 202

—R—

Rahner, Karl, vii, 9, 12-13, 42-43, 46-47, 49-51, 53, 64-66, 82, 98, 105, 112, 119, 121-123, 144, 148, 150, 156
Ratzinger, Joseph, 149, 179
Realsymbol (e), 51, 53, 150
relationship, vi-vii, 1-3, 6-7, 15-17, 25, 34, 43-44, 46-47, 51, 53, 58, 61, 70, 75, 89, 91, 95, 97, 109, 116, 120, 123-124, 129, 133, 137, 152, 161, 165-166, 177-178, 184, 186, 191-192, 202, 204

revelation, i, v-viii, xii, xv, xvii, 1-
9, 18-23, 27, 29-42, 46-49, 51-
65, 69-158, 162-178, 180-182,
184-186, 188, 190, 193-195,
199-200, 204-209, 211-217
social dimensions of, 84, 96, 115
symbolic dimensions of, vii, 115
symbolic mediation of, ix, 178,
183, 192, 194
symbolic structure of, 113, 151
Ricœur, Paul, 62

—S—

Schleiermacher, Friedrich, 21
Segundo, Juan Luis, 79
sensus fidelium, viii, 28, 80, 135-
136, 139, 185, 195, 197
sign, 52, 67, 99, 101, 109, 124,
147, 152, 155
socialization, 157-158, 165, 196-
197
Soukop, Paul A., 71
symbol, vii, viii, 7, 9, 11-12, 15,
37, 40, 46, 49-57, 59-67, 74-76,
82, 85, 87, 90, 93-99, 101, 103-
108, 110, 113-118, 124, 127-
128, 132-134, 142, 144-146,
149-150, 152, 155, 162, 168,
173, 194, 197-199, 203
nature of, viii, 54, 60, 109
ontology of, vii, 49-50, 65-66
participatory knowledge, viii, 57-
59, 62, 73, 75, 88, 169
presentative, 53, 150, 162
realizing, 105
tensive, 52
symbolic realism, 37, 82, 102-103,
105-106, 108, 110-111, 123,
127-128, 143, 154, 199
symbolic reality, 53, 66, 98-99,
103, 150

—T—

tacit knowing, 90, 129
Thompson, William M., 168
Tillard, Jean M. R., 168
Tillich, Paul, 62, 66, 94, 171
Tracy, David, 178
tradition, 2, 4-6, 11, 15, 17, 24-25,
79, 102, 104, 108-109, 113,
117, 120, 124, 131, 135, 137,
138-139, 144, 147, 149-150,
155-156, 158-161, 163, 165-
169, 171-173, 175-187, 190-
192, 194-195, 197, 199, 203
scripture and, 173, 178
traditioning, 157-158, 164-166,
169, 171, 179, 182, 187, 201
traditions, 165, 176, 179, 180,
182, 192, 194, 205

—U—

Urban, Wilbur M., 107, 122

—V—

Vatican Council I, xv, 43, 71, 94-
95, 147-148, 150-151, 156,
159-160, 163, 165-166, 169,
172, 177, 179, 181-185
Vatican Council II, xv, 43, 71, 148,
151, 156, 159-160, 163, 165-
166, 169, 172, 177, 179, 181-
185
Vertretungssymbol (e), 51, 53, 150
Vorgriff, 101, 123

—W—

Word of God, 36, 146
Wheelwright, Philip, 52